D0876255

WORK
ALIENATION

WORK ALIENATION

An Integrative Approach

Rabindra N. Kanungo

PRAEGER SPECIAL STUDIES • PRAEGER SCIENTIFIC

Library of Congress Cataloging in Publication Data

Kanungo, Rabindra Nath.
  Work alienation.

    Includes index.
    1. Job satisfaction.   2. Alienation (Social psy-
chology)   3. Psychology, Industrial.   I. Title.
HF5549.5.J63K36   158.7   81-20959
ISBN 0-03-060241-6   AACR2

Published in 1982 by Praeger Publishers
CBS Educational and Professional Publishing
a Division of CBS Inc.
521 Fifth Avenue, New York, New York 10175, U.S.A.

© 1982 by Praeger Publishers

23456789   145   987654321

Printed in the United States of America

To Mom and Dad,

who taught me to live for a career,

and

to Lunik and Mig,

who taught me to work for a living

PREFACE

This book grew out of my disagreement and discontent with the existing conventional wisdom regarding the phenomena of work alienation and involvement. My disagreements and discontent are not with the need for better understanding of the phenomena, in which case writing this book would have been superfluous; rather, the disagreements and discontent expressed in the book stem from the existing conceptualization and measurement of the phenomena.

Everybody, social scientists and management practitioners alike, is keenly aware of the necessity of having a clear grasp of the phenomena of work alienation and involvement. No one disagrees that the phenomena play a central role in determining the social and economic climates of contemporary postindustrial societies. Understanding the phenomena, their causes, and consequences, is considered vital for improving the quality of life for workers and the effectiveness of the organizations in which they work. Realizing the importance of the phenomena for the workers and organizations, psychologists and sociologists have empirically studied the phenomena for the last three decades, but their studies have resulted in piecemeal and culturally biased theories and contradictory findings with questionable cross-cultural generalizability. Increasing numbers of studies on work alienation in recent years have introduced increasing amounts of confusion and vagueness, rather than clarity, to our understanding. There have been very small attempts at parsimony and integration of concepts describing the phenomena in these studies. Very often the conceptual bases of these studies are of questionable validity and limited generalizability. The results of these studies, because of the use of faulty measurement techniques, have often perpetuated many myths, rather than facts. Dispelling these myths with the help of a cross-culturally valid, integrative-conceptual framework and development of appropriate measurement techniques for use in future research are the major objectives of this book. Hopefully, the book will put to rest many culturally biased and faulty conceptions regarding the nature of work ethics and job involvement and their impact on individuals and organizations. The new integrative-conceptual approach and the new measurement techniques suggested in the book will provide fresh directions for future research. Eventually, out of such research a clearer and more systematic understanding of the phenomenon of work alienation across different cultures will emerge.

Writing a book that attacks conventional wisdom is always a difficult task for a single person. Without many of my colleagues, the task simply could not have been accomplished. I am grateful to all of them. However, my special thanks go to Jon Hartwick, Moses Kiggundu, and Alex Whitmore for their valuable criticisms and suggestions. Special thanks are also due Natarajan Rajan, who worked with me throughout the whole project and helped me immensely in data analysis and interpretation. Two of my research assistants, Tejbir Singh Phool and Glen Board, assisted me in the preparation of the manuscript, and I am thankful to them. I am very much indebted to Jean Hepworth for her untiring efforts in typing and proofreading several drafts of the manuscript. Finally, my wife, Minati, deserves special credit for her patience and understanding during the time I was courting the book.

Partial support for several studies reported in the book came from the Department of Education, Government of Quebec, and the Faculty of Management, McGill University. Grateful acknowledgment is made to those agencies. Acknowledgments are also due to the Academic Press, the American Psychological Association, the Academy of Management Journal, and the MIT Press for their kind permission to reproduce certain previously published materials.

CONTENTS

LIST OF TABLES

LIST OF FIGURES

WORK
ALIENATION

1

INTRODUCTION

The advent of the alienated man and all the themes which
lie behind his advent now affect the whole of our serious
intellectual life and cause our immediate intellectual
malaise.

C. Wright Mills, 1959

ON THE IMPORTANCE OF STUDYING ALIENATION

The study of work alienation is important for three reasons.
The first reason is a theoretical one: lack of conceptual clarity with
respect to the usage of the term alienation suggests the need for theoretical refinement of the concept. The other two reasons have a
more pragmatic flavor. The study of alienation is important because
it will provide a better understanding of how to improve the quality of
life of individual employees on the one hand and organizational effectiveness on the other. Let us consider each of the three reasons
separately.

There is a need for understanding the meaning of the concept
"alienation" and its obverse "involvement" in unequivocal terms.
Johnson (1973a) aptly describes the term alienation as "an atrocious
word. In its use as a general concept, scientific term, popular expression, and cultural motif, alienation has acquired a semantic richness (and confusion) attained by few words of corresponding significance in contemporary parlance" (p. 3). If one scans through the social science literature of the past two decades, one encounters numerous usages of the concepts of alienation and involvement. These
concepts have been used by sociologists, psychologists, political scientists, theologians, philosophers, and historians to describe and
explain various contemporary social phenomena. In fact, the terms

1

alienation and involvement have been used so often and in so many contexts that they have acquired an aura of equivocality. As Seeman (1971) pointed out, the concept of alienation has been "popularly adopted as the signature of the present epoch. It has become routine to define our troubles in the language of alienation and to seek solutions in those terms. But signatures are sometimes hard to read, sometimes spurious, and sometimes too casually and promiscuously used. They ought to be examined with care" (p. 135). Similar concern was expressed by Johnson (1973b), who characterized the concept of alienation as being capable of carrying a great deal of feeling "in an inexplicit, perplexing and deeply annoying way" (p. 28). Although in recent years many psychologists and sociologists have attempted to demystify and operationalize the concept (Lawler and Hall 1970; Lodahl and Kejner 1965; Saleh and Hosek 1976; Seeman 1971; Vroom 1962), none of them seem to offer a scientifically organized and meaningful view of the concept that could have broad generality across cultures.

Lack of cross-cultural generality of the existing conceptualizations of the phenomena of alienation and involvement has been treated at some length in the subsequent chapters of this book. However, let me briefly mention it here to sensitize the readers to the issue. Consider, for example, the manner in which most social scientists have interpreted the notions of work alienation and involvement. Following Marx (1932), most social scientists have viewed work alienation as resulting from the lack of opportunity within organizations to satisfy workers' needs for personal control, autonomy, and self-actualization. The modern organization with its bureaucratic structure, its formal rules and regulations, its impersonal climate, and its mechanized, routine operations, is accused of creating conditions for the loss of individuality that results in a state of alienation in workers. Besides the influence of the working environment in a postindustrial society, work alienation is often considered as an absence of the Protestant work ethic, as advocated by Weber (1930). The critical elements of the Protestant work ethic are the qualities of individualism and a form of asceticism. The reason for an emphasis on the quality of individualism stems from the Protestant faith that "God helps those who help themselves." The quality of asceticism was emphasized because of the Calvanistic preaching that work is its own reward; that one should believe in the intrinsic aspect of work; that one must value work not because work brings an external reward, but because work is the best use of one's time and is intrinsically satisfying; and that work should be engaged in for its own sake. Lack of faith in the Protestant work ethic and in the qualities of individualism and asceticism lead to the alienation of man from work. Such interpretations pervade most of Western thinking on the subject. The operationalization of the concepts is based on these interpretations.

But one can argue that the Western conceptualizations and measurements may be culture specific to the extent that their validity and applicability in other non-Western societies may be questionable. For instance, one might raise questions, such as, Is it necessary to equate the Protestant work ethic with work involvement? Is it necessary to promote individualism in order to achieve greater worker involvement? Is it reasonable to argue that societies that do not subscribe to the Protestant work ethic and, therefore, do not value individualism and work asceticism harbor only alienated workers? Is it not true that the Protestant work ethic is the product of a specific religious doctrine of Western Europe and has dominated the intellectual tradition of people in North America? Can the extent of work alienation or the involvement of people belonging to other parts of the world be assessed by standards developed in a specific cultural context? These questions raise doubts about the present conceptualizations of alienation and also argue for a fresh look and a reformulation of the issue. Developing a reformulation that has the potentiality for pancultural application has been a major objective of this book.

Most of the researchers have tried to explain the phenomena of alienation and involvement in social-psychological terms (Clark 1959; Lawler and Hall 1970; Seeman 1959). But the language they have used seems to have created more confusion than clarity. Sociological and psychological explanations of the phenomena seem to run parallel courses of their own without any serious attempt at integration. In fact, if one puts together the various explanations of the phenomena advanced by these writers, one ends up with greater conceptual fuzziness, rather than clarity or understanding. If we take seriously Seeman's (1971) call for a careful examination of the concepts for better clarity and rigor, we ought to seek a reformulation of the issue. This book presents such a reformulation of the issue and provides arguments in favor of some theoretical and methodological refinements.

The second reason for the study of alienation is to appreciate better the nature of an individual's alienating experiences at work and how such experiences affect one's life in general. The terms work alienation or work involvement are often used to describe and explain salient features of an individual's life experiences in contemporary societies. For instance, the experience of alienation from work has been described by Jenkins (1973) as a schizoid condition. Jenkins considers an alienated worker as one who when

subjected to the stress of "a threatening experience from which there is no physical escape" develops an elaborate protective mechanism; "he becomes a mental observer, who looks on, detached and impassive at what his body is doing or what is being done to his body." For that person, "the world is a prison without bars, a concentration camp without barbed wire." Instead of experiencing reality directly, he develops a "false" self as a buffer for the real world, while the real self retires to an "inner" position of unexposed safety. All of life seems full of "futility, meaninglessness, and purposelessness," since it is not, in fact, being directly experienced. The real self is completely blocked, barred from any spontaneous expression or real freedom of action and totally sterile. In the absence of a spontaneous, natural, creative relationship with the world which is free from anxiety, the "inner self" thus develops an overall sense of inner impoverishment, which is experienced in complaints of the emptiness, deadness, coldness, dryness, impotence, desolation, worthlessness, of the inner life. [P. 43]

Likewise, commenting on the life experience of an alienated factory worker, Tocqueville (1961) observes the following:

When a workman is unceasingly and exclusively engaged in the fabrication of one thing, he ultimately does his work with singular dexterity; but at the same time he loses the general faculty of applying his mind to the direction of the work. He every day becomes more adroit and less industrious; so that it may be said of him, that in proportion as the workman improves the man is degraded. . . . When a workman has spent a considerable portion of his existence in this manner, his thoughts are forever set upon the object of his daily toil; his body has contracted certain fixed habits, which it can never shake off: in a word, he no longer belongs to himself, but to the calling which he has chosen. . . . In proportion as the principle of the division of labour is more extensively applied, the workman becomes more weak, more narrow-minded and more dependent. [Pp. 190-91]

These are examples of qualitative descriptions of states of alienation. Can these states of an individual's experiences be operationalized? Can states of alienation and involvement be measured? Does alienation from work pervade other aspects of one's life (for example, family and community)? Is the widely accepted Marxian dictum that work alienation is the cause of all other social problems in life true? Is work alienation the result of a declining Protestant work ethic? Or is it the result of mass-production technology? Clearly these are important questions that need to be answered before one can attempt to bring about improvements in an individual's quality of life both on and off the job.

Finally, in the area of human-resource management, the persistent problem faced by managers is how to improve organizational effectiveness through the proper utilization of human resources. The major hurdle in proper utilization of human resources stems from alienating attitudes of employees. Employee alienation manifests itself in various forms and at all levels within an organization. Instances of blue-collar blues and salaried dropouts are quite common. Worker apathy, deliberate sabotage, high rates of absenteeism among all categories of employees, union strikes, and work-to-order campaigns are all too numerous. They constantly threaten the very existence of modern organizations. All these organizational evils are often considered as a manifestation of the employees' alienation from work. If the underlying experience of alienation is the root of major problems in organizations, then one must understand the nature of work alienation. For such understanding, one must find answers to the following questions: What is the nature of the alienating experience of employees? What are its causes and effects? How can one diagnose the state of work alienation? Can alienation be measured in operational terms? Can one predict and prevent alienation among employees? This book deals with these questions and attempts to provide some answers. In the process of dealing with these issues, several other questions are raised that need to be resolved in future research.

GENERAL PLAN OF THE BOOK

The three reasons for studying work alienation provide the rationale for the topics discussed in this book. The major objectives of the book are fourfold. First, the book attempts to provide a critical assessment of the state of the art and theory concerning work alienation. In trying to meet this objective, Chapter 2 provides a very broad historical perspective on the concept of alienation. The chapter points out the major rational and empirical traditions in the treatment of alienation and involvement as important social phenomena. Chapters 3 and 4 focus more specifically on the sociological and psychological approaches to alienation and involvement. Both of these approaches exemplify the current empirical tradition in the social sciences for the study of social phenomena. Therefore, the chapters deal with both the theoretical and methodological developments in their respective areas. Chapter 5 presents a critical assessment of these approaches. In doing so, several conceptual and measurement problems associated with these approaches are identified. Furthermore, a review of psychological and sociological approaches to alienation suggests the existence of two unrelated parallel streams of thought that require proper integration. After identifying these problems, the requirements for a reformulation of the concepts and for some refinements in measurement are suggested.

This brings us to the second objective of the book, which is to provide a new approach to the study of alienation. Chapter 6 presents a new formulation describing the underlying dynamics of and a comprehensive conceptual framework for the study of the phenomena of alienation and involvement. The framework aims at integrating the sociological and psychological thinking on each issue and provides a more complete understanding of the complex phenomena in a parsimonious way.

The third objective of the book is to provide ways of measuring the phenomena of alienation and involvement. Development of such measurement techniques are described in Chapter 7. Comparative analyses are done among the various existing and new measures on the basis of their construct validity and cross-cultural applicability.

The final objective of the book is to provide information on the criterion-related validity of the new formulation for the study of the phenomena of alienation and involvement. Such information is contained in Chapter 8. Several studies reported on in Chapter 8 provide a better understanding of the role of work and person-related variables in employee alienation and involvement. Since the theoretical framework for the study of alienation presented in this book is relatively new, much more research needs to be done in the future to test predictions derived from the theory. Thus, new directions for future research and new applications in organizational settings are indicated in the final chapter.

2

A HISTORICAL
PERSPECTIVE

Every society is tempted to regard itself as unique, as
something new under the sun, as facing problems never
seen before. But every society, if it wishes for wisdom,
should consult the experience of its ancestors.

David Herlihy, 1973

Contemporary social scientists often consider work alienation
as a distinctly post-Reformation or postindustrial phenomenon. For
instance, Faunce (1968) suggests that the characteristics of an industrial society, such as economic affluence, rapidly changing industrial
technology, ever increasing size and complexity of social organizations, and rapid social change, have resulted in the alienation of workers in our society. Faunce states his views in the following way:

Loneliness in the midst of urban agglomeration; loss of
social anchorage in mass society; the absence of a predictable life trajectory in an era of unprecedented social
change; and the powerlessness of man within the complex
social, economic, and political systems he has created
are common themes in the social criticism of the industrial way of life. Concern with alienated quality of existence is particularly widespread today since poverty,
which was once the major target of social critics, has
become less common. However, alienation has been
recognized and condemned as a product of industrialism
almost from the time of the initial disruption of traditional ways during the Industrial Revolution. [P. 84]

The contention that work alienation is a postindustrial phenomenon, however, is generally disputed by theologians, philosophers,

7

and historians. These scholars claim that work alienation as a social phenomenon or human experience has existed throughout the recorded history of humankind. Whether in the Dark Ages when magic and mysticism influenced the productive efforts of individuals for maintaining their existence or in the Middle Ages when an individual's work life was deeply influenced by medieval religious beliefs and practices, human beings in their work lives have experienced alienation perhaps just as much as they experience it in the modern, post-industrial, machine civilization. Work alienation has existed in all ages; however, the nature of its manifestation has changed from time to time because of changes in societal and technological contexts. Slave and peasant revolts of ancient times have been substituted by strike and work-to-rule campaigns of organized labor today.

Johnson (1973a) pointed out that social alienation as an observed phenomenon is quite ancient and the term alienation is an antique one. Theologians take credit for using the term as an explanatory concept. Alienation, according to them, refers to states of separation of human beings from God, from their own bodies, from their fellow human beings, and from their institutions. This interpretation is clearly reflected in the use of dualism of body and soul in theological writings. Essentially, the theologians observed and explained the meaninglessness of human existence in terms of spiritual alienation or separation from God and moral principles. Although alienation as a psychological state of the individual (or as a collective social phenomenon) has been recognized for centuries, the scientific treatment of the concept with regard to its nature and its effects was attempted first by empirically oriented sociologists and, more recently, by social psychologists. Thus, the concept has lived through two distinct traditions, the rational and the empirical. The rational tradition of the concept comes largely from the writings of theologians (Macquarrie 1973) and philosophers (Denise 1973). The empirical tradition results from the recent works of sociologists and psychologists. Most contemporary formulations by both sociologists and psychologists on the subject of work alienation are based on the intellectual foundations laid by the early writings of theologians and philosophers. Therefore, our present-day understanding, as well as our confusions regarding the concept of alienation, owe a great deal to the early theological and philosophical treatises on this subject. The purpose of this chapter is to present an overview of the early theological and philosophical views that provide the intellectual background of the concept. For a more detailed discussion of the rational tradition, the reader is referred to the work of Richard Schacht (1970).

LINGUISTIC ORIGIN OF THE TERM <u>ALIENATION</u>

The English term <u>alienation</u> is derived from the original Latin noun <u>alienatio,</u> which in turn is derived from the Latin verb <u>alienare</u> meaning to "take away" or "remove" (Klein 1966). The Latin usage of the term in different contexts, however, resulted in two distinct meanings of the concept. The first meaning was derived from the Latin usage of the term in the context of transfer of ownership of property. In this context, the use of the term <u>alienation</u> meant the "transfer of ownership of something to another person." In the fifteenth century, such usage of the term was quite common. Even today, the term is sometimes used in political, economic, and legal contexts to mean the transfer of property from one person to another. The second meaning of alienation was derived from the Latin usage of the verb <u>alienare</u> meaning "to cause a separation to occur." In this sense alienation referred to "a state of separation or dissociation" (Klein 1966) between two elements.

THEOLOGICAL USAGE OF THE TERM <u>ALIENATION</u>

The second meaning of alienation as a state of separation was primarily popularized in early theological writings. For this reason, the <u>Middle English Dictionary</u> (Kurath and Kuhn 1956) identified the usage of the term as "chiefly theological." The term is used in the Bible; Paul characterizes the gentiles as "darkened in their understanding, alienated from the life of God (Ephesians 4:18). Calvin (1854) used the term <u>alienation</u> in a commentary on spiritual death. According to Calvin, "spiritual death is nothing else than alienation of the soul from God . . ." (p. 219). In these passages, the term <u>alienation</u> was used to mean a state of separation from God. Not only in Christianity but also in Hinduism and Buddhism spiritual alienation has been interpreted as a state of separation or dissociation from God. Most theologians found the cause of spiritual alienation in worldly (material and sensuous) involvement. In order to avoid spiritual alienation, they encouraged alienation from the physical and social world. Thus, primitive Christianity preached that the world belonged to the devil, nature was the enemy, and the body was a prison. Likewise, the "sages of the Upanishads sought to estrange their disciples from nature, from society, from their own bodies. . . (Kaufmann 1970, p. liv). The theologians advocated the desirability of work alienation if work was a means to satisfy personal material (physical), social, or ego needs. In Hindu scripture (Bhagavad Gita), karma (work) was considered desirable only when it was performed as a pure sense of duty without any attachment to its outcomes or without any desire for personal gains.

The term alienation, when defined as a state of separation, always implied two additional features. First, an individual must experience a state of alienation from some other element, person, or thing. In dealing with states of alienation in the spiritual life of individuals, theological approaches emphasized the idea that there can be alienation of different sorts, depending on what elements of one's environment one is separated from (such as God, one's own body, or other people). Following a similar line of reasoning, the social scientists of today talk of different kinds of alienation, such as job alienation, organizational alienation, urban alienation, and family alienation. From the point of view of conducting empirical research, social scientists consider the study of alienation in relation to single, well-defined environmental elements (such as job or family) to be more fruitful than the study of alienation in a global sense (Clark 1959; Seeman 1971).

The meaning of alienation as a state of separation contained a second feature. An individual in a state of separation from an object was assumed to experience a certain affect toward the object. The term alienation, therefore, always had a reference to the individual's affective experience associated with a state of separation. An alienated individual was generally perceived as showing cool, aversive, hostile, or unwelcome feelings (Klein 1966; Murray 1888) toward the object of alienation. In theological writings, the negative affective states of despair, guilt, dissatisfaction, anger, and so on were considered common manifestations of spiritual alienation. The inclusion of negative affective states as a part of the phenomenon of alienation can also be noticed in the writings of contemporary social scientists. The negative affective states of dissatisfaction and hostility among workers have been described by sociologists and psychologists as indicators of the state of alienation from work.

USAGE OF THE TERM ALIENATION
IN POLITICAL THEORY

The meaning of the term alienation as a "transfer of ownership" (one of the two meanings derived from Latin usage) was largely used by social-contract theorists such as Grotius, Hobbes, Locke, and Rousseau. Hugo Grotius (1853) was the first social-contract theorist to use the Latin term alienatio to mean the transfer of "sovereign authority" over oneself to another person. According to Grotius, transferring the right of self-determination to someone else is like a transfer of ownership of property. For Grotius such alienation represents limits to individual autonomy and freedom of action and forms the basis of all political authority. Other social-contract theorists, such as Thomas Hobbes (1950) and John Locke (1947), have not used the term alienation, but have expressed views similar to those of Grotius. For instance, Hobbes used the words "renouncing" or "transferring" one's "rights" or "liberty" while entering the social contract to establish political authority. Likewise, Locke spoke of "resigning up" or "quitting" certain powers and putting them in the hands of the community for better civil government. Rousseau (1947), in his social-contract theory, used the term alienation to mean the total surrender of an individual's person and power to the collective general will. According to Rousseau, a social contract requires that "each of us contributes to the group his person and the powers which he wields as a person under the supreme direction of the general will, and we receive into the body politic each individual as forming an indivisible part of the whole" (p. 257). Thus, the meaning of alienation was extended from a transfer of certain individual rights to the complete surrender of the entire person.

In social-contract theories, an alienated worker was one who gave up or surrendered personal "rights," "liberty," "powers," and "controls" to the general will of the community or organization. Such alienation of the worker, however, was viewed as desirable because social–contract theorists assumed that the long-term gains from a social contract would outweigh the personal loss of rights and liberties.

HEGEL'S USE OF THE TERM ALIENATION

According to Erich Fromm (1941, 1966), it was Hegel who put the concept of alienation on an analytic footing and, along with Marx, laid the intellectual foundation for the understanding of the problem of alienation in modern society. Hegel used alienation in the two different ways discussed in the preceding paragraphs. Hegel was influenced by Rousseau's discussion of alienation as a "surrender" of personal self and control. He was also influenced by the writings of other German philosophers, such as Friedrich Schiller (1954), who retained the theological usage of alienation, meaning a state of separation. Such influences led Hegel to use two distinct German words, entausserung (meaning "surrender" or "divestiture") and entfremdung (meaning a "state of separation") for describing the dual nature of alienation. In his book, Philosophy of Rights, Hegel (1942) used the term entausserung in the specific contexts of property transfer and labor contract. However, he used both entausserung and entfremdung

interchangeably as different forms of alienation in his book, Phenomenology of Mind (1949).

According to Hegel (1949), there are two types of alienation.
First, there is the conscious experience of alienation as a state of
separation. One experiences this type of alienation when one ceases
to identify with the "social substance" or the social, political, and
cultural institutions. This type of alienation or state of separation
refers to "a condition which occurs when a certain change in a person's self-conception takes place. It is neither something one does
nor the intended result of a deliberate action" (Schacht 1970, p. 36).
It is rather a state of consciousness reflecting a condition of separation that has come to exist for the individual. The second type of
alienation refers to the surrender or transfer of individual rights.
In contrast to the first type of alienation, surrendering one's rights
is something deliberate. "It involves a conscious relinquishment or
surrender with the intention of securing a desired end: namely, unity
with the social substance" (Schacht 1970, p. 36). Hegel considers
the conscious state of separation from the social substance (alienation
in the first sense) as an undesirable state for the individual. He suggests that such alienation be overcome through continuous and deliberate relinquishment or surrender of one's personal interests.
Thus, the second type of alienation (as deliberate surrender), according to Hegel, is very desirable.

In discussing the problem of alienation, Hegel presents an
idealistic point of view. In the work context, Hegel's arguments
would imply that alienation or separation from work, organization,
and job (components of the social substance in Hegelian terms) is not
desirable. In order to overcome such alienation, workers should
make personal sacrifices. The interests of the total work organization should be valued more than interests of the individual workers.
The latter has to be sacrificed to achieve the former. But one may
raise two issues here. First, why should workers sacrifice their
personal interests and desires for achieving unity (involvement or
identity) with work and work organizations? Second, how effective
will such sacrifices be for the desired goal of achieving unity? Contemporary theories about human nature and motivation would suggest
that sacrifices of personal desires will generally result in greater
separation than unity. As Schacht (1970) pointed out, "The idea of
so considerable a relinquishment of independence and a subordination of particularity to universality is not likely to be as acceptable
to most people today as it was to Hegel" (p. 48).

MARX'S USE OF THE TERM ALIENATION

Karl Marx (1963) provided the most elaborate treatment of work
alienation and strongly influenced contemporary thinking on the sub-

ject. Marx followed Hegel's philosophical treatment of the concept of alienation but carved a place for it in political economy, rather than in philosophy. If Hegel, following theologians and philosophers of his time, identified the basic psychological state of alienation in individuals' spiritual lives, Marx identified it in their material working lives. Thus, Marx spoke of alienation of labor, rather than spiritual alienation. However, the two meanings of alienation (separation and surrender) used in Hegel's analysis were the starting point for Marx in his interpretation of alienation of labor.

Hegel's (1949) notion of the "universal essence of man," as discussed in the Phenomenology of Mind, influenced Marx's thinking on human nature. Hegel proposed that there is a universal essence of man that, when realized (through developing unity with social substance), results in the self-fulfillment of mankind. Marx also believed in the essential nature of human beings, but for the most part referred to it in terms of productive activity or labor. Labor, according to Marx (1932), represents "existential activity of man, his free conscious activity—not as a means for maintaining life but for developing his universal nature" (pp. 87-88). Marx identified two other aspects of the essential nature of human beings besides labor and spontaneous, free, self-directed productive activities of individuals. These two aspects were social existence (in fellowship with other human beings) and sensuous existence (cultivation and enjoyment of the senses). "Thus for Marx, man's essential characteristics are those of individuality, sociality, and sensuousness. For Hegel, they are those of individuality and universality" (Schacht 1970, p. 74). For Marx, labor alienation represents a loss of individuality or separation of individuals from their labor. Erich Fromm (1966) describes Marx's view of alienation or separation from labor. "Alienation (or 'estrangement') means, for Marx, that man does not experience himself as the acting agent in his grasp of the world, but that the world (nature, others, and he himself) remains alien to him. They stand above and against him as objects, even though they may be objects of his own creation. Alienation is essentially experiencing the world and oneself passively, receptively, as the subject separated from the object" (p. 44). For Marx separation caused by a loss of individuality blocks the realization of the essential or universal nature of human beings and is, therefore, undesirable. For Hegel, on the other hand, loss of individuality is a means to realize an identity with the universal nature and is, therefore, desirable. Although Marx, unlike Hegel, viewed alienation owing to a loss of individuality as essentially an undesirable state, he retained the Hegelian use of the notion of separation or dissociation in his treatment of alienation.

Marx was also influenced by Hegel's treatment of alienation as a "surrender of rights." Hegel (1942) discussed the relationship between property and personality in his book <u>Philosophy of Rights</u>. According to Hegel, property or taking possession of things is an embodiment of one's freedom and personality. Individuals acquire property through a productive or "forming" activity. Since productive activity reflects one's will and personality, the product of such activity is the objectification of individuals. Following Hegel closely, Marx (1963) also considered production as "the direct activity of individuality" (p. 157) and referred to this process as a form of "externalization." Through such externalization, workers achieve self-realization. According to Marx, workers, through their own labor, fulfill themselves and develop freely their spiritual and physical energies. Workers can consider their labor as truly their own (in the sense of property ownership) only when their labor reflects their needs, interests, and free will, and manifests their personalities. If workers sacrifice their needs and interests and surrender their free will or control over what they do, they experience alienation. For Marx, the mechanization of the production process and supervisory control under the capitalist system forces workers to surrender their rights to engage in spontaneous, free, and self-directed productive activities and, thus, creates alienation of labor.

It may be noticed from the above discussion that Marx borrowed the two meanings of alienation (cognitive state of separation and acts of surrender of rights) directly from Hegel, but fused them together to form one general meaning to represent the psychological state of alienation. For Marx, the alienation of workers refers to a state of separation from labor (and products of labor) caused by the surrender of workers' natural rights (or desires for autonomy and control). As Schacht (1970) so aptly put it, "In Marx, Hegel's two senses of 'alienation' come together, and a single general sense emerges, which may be characterized as 'separation through surrender. . . .' In Marx, the separation is the result of surrender; whereas in Hegel's discussion of the relation of the individual to the social substance the separation is overcome through the surrender" (p. 83).

The fusion of the two meanings of alienation by Marx has strongly influenced contemporary social scientists. Following Marx, most social scientists assumed that the absence of worker autonomy and control at the work place are the necessary and sufficient conditions of labor alienation. Such an assumption is based on the uncritical acceptance of Marxian views regarding labor and the essence of human nature. The validity of the assumption, however, can be questioned on the ground that the essential nature of human beings and the role of labor in a worker's life as conceived by Marx may not hold true. In light of current behavioral and motivational theories, Marxian emphasis on worker autonomy and control appears very humanistic in its orientation and, like many assumptions in humanistic psychology (such as Maslow's need-hierarchy notion), may suffer from problems of empirical validation.

At this point, Marxian views on labor and human nature may be critically examined in social-psychological terms in order to highlight Marx's humanistic orientation and its influence on contemporary sociological and psychological thinking. Marx (1932) thought of labor or working on a job as the "spontaneous," "free," "conscious," "self-directed," and "existential activity" of man. For Marx, labor was not a means of maintaining physical existence, but for developing a "universal nature." Thus, a state of work involvement ideally results when the work situation elicits job behavior that is perceived to be voluntary; not instrumental in satisfying basic physical needs; instrumental in satisfying Maslow-type (1954) higher-order needs, such as the need for self-realization or self-actualization; and conducive to developing individuals' abilities to their fullest potential. In the absence of such perceptions, the workers are bound to experience a state of alienation from work. In this respect Marx's thinking is very similar to the humanistic orientation of modern organization theorists (for example, McGregor 1960).

Most postindustrial work settings, according to Marx, provide job conditions that alienate workers, rather than involve them. Marx identified two major job conditions that are responsible for alienation among workers. They are the separation of workers from the products of their labor and the separation of workers from the means of production. The first job condition implies that the product is perceived as not belonging to the workers. The workers also perceive that they cannot influence the disposition or quality of the product. Thus, they lack a sense of ownership and control over the product and its quality. The second job condition implies that the workers perceive a lack of control over the function of the machines and other means of production. Finding that they have no control over their working lives, workers are bound to be estranged or to separate their working lives from the rest of their existence, over which Marx assumes the workers have complete control.

The Marxian concept of alienation not only implies a lack of control, autonomy, and ownership over one's job, it also implies submission of labor to the direction of another person (subordination). Schacht (1970) pointed out that such conceptualization suffers from the problems of both over- and underinclusiveness. For instance, working under supervisory direction (as in the case of a member of a research team) does not necessarily preclude self-fulfillment and, therefore, is not necessarily alienating. "Labor performed under the direction of another man thus need not be 'alien activity.' To conceive 'alienated labor' in these terms, therefore, is to render the concept too inclusive" (Schacht 1970, p. 92).

Worker alienation conceived in terms of lack of control and autonomy is also not inclusive enough. If one translates the alienation state of the worker into motivational terms, it becomes quite clear that Marx intended to measure alienation in terms of the lack of fulfillment of a single set of needs, the ego needs for independence, achievement, and power. But it is quite possible that the worker may experience work alienation when other physical and social needs are not met on the job.

In the Marxian formulation, the role of other human needs, such as the physical and the social ones, has been completely disregarded, as if such needs to not constitute a part of one's self or perhaps constitute a very insignificant part exerting almost no influence in causing work alienation. This interpretation of the Marxian formulation may appear oversimplified, but it is clearly reflected in the following quotation from Marx:

> What constitutes alienation of labor? First, that work is external to the worker, that it is not part of his nature; and that, consequently, he does not fulfill himself in his work but denies himself, has a feeling of misery rather than than well-being, does not develop freely his mental and physical energies but is physically exhausted and mentally debased. The worker therefore feels himself at home only during his leisure time, whereas at work he feels homeless. His work is not voluntary but imposed, forced labor. It is not the satisfaction of a need, but only a means for satisfying other needs. [Pp. 85-86]

Clearly, Marx considered labor only as productive activity when it is meant to satisfy the intrinsic needs of workers. Labor has no end to achieve other than this. "It is therefore a perversion of its essential function, according to Marx, when it is undertaken merely 'under the compulsion of direct physical needs' or that 'selfish need' which he terms 'greed'" (Schacht 1970, p. 93). One may notice the assumptions Marx makes while defining the state of labor alienation. It is obvious that he emphasizes the worker's experience of frustration over autonomy and control needs at work, and whenever these needs are frustrated, Marx considers work to be external to the worker's self. He even goes further to suggest that the payment of money for labor cannot reduce alienation. When labor "is regarded as something to be exchanged for pay, 'labor appears not as an end in itself but as the servant of wages,' and thus loses its 'human significance and worth.' Here it 'is not the satisfaction of a need, but only a means for satisfying other needs.' It is unimportant whether these 'other needs' are 'physical needs' or 'selfish needs'; in both cases, labor is pressed into the service of needs other than that of self-realization" (Schacht 1970, p. 93).

Another assumption made by Marx is revealed in the above quotation. The assumption is related to the instrumental and consummatory properties of job behavior. According to Marx, job behavior can be either instrumental activity that satisfies basic physical and selfish human needs, or it can be the final consummatory activity. In the former sense, job behavior is viewed as the means to an end (satisfaction of extrinsic needs), and in the latter sense it is viewed as an end in itself. Theories of human motivation suggest that human behavior is purposive, has directionality, is initiated by need states, and is always instrumental in satisfying these need states. An individual's job behavior is also purposive; it is aimed at satisfying both the extrinsic- and intrinsic-need states (Lawler 1973) of the individual. However, when Marx wrote of job behavior as an end in itself (reflecting a state of involvement), he did not recognize that such behavior is also instrumental in satisfying a set of intrinsic human needs. In order to be consistent with current psychological theories, labor as a a form of human activity has to be viewed as instrumental (and not consummatory) in satisfying different needs (extrinsic or intrinsic) of workers. Some workers try to satisfy their need for money and others try to satisfy their need for personal achievement through labor or work activities. In both cases labor is a productive activity. No one works just for the sake of work without an underlying personal need to initiate purposive work activity.

SUMMARY

The contributions of early theologians, social-contract theorists, and philosophers, specifically Hegel and Marx, provide the intellectual background and the rational tradition of the concept of alienation. It is quite evident that there is a historical continuity in the development of the two original meanings of alienation in Latin usage (separation and surrender). In the work of Marx these two meanings converged to explain labor alienation as a form of separation from work through the frustration of a worker's intrinsic needs. The emphasis on the satisfaction of the intrinsic needs of workers as a necessary condition of work involvement (as implied in Marx's writings) is a reflection of Marx's humanistic and cultural background and is questionable on the basis of current psychological theories of human behavior. However, as will be noticed in the next two chapters, Marx's influence in this regard has persisted up to the present time in the empirical literature on the subject. Although it is not quite apparent on the surface, a closer examination will reveal that many confusions in the empirical literature on work alienation have resulted from adopting the Marxian rational treatment of work alienation.

3

THE SOCIOLOGICAL APPROACH

In the nineteenth century the problem was that God is dead;
in the twentieth century the problem is that man is dead.
Erich Fromm, 1955

The contributions of sociologists in explaining the nature of
alienation have been the most extensive. Armed with the intellectual
background provided by Marx, sociologists have sought to explain the
maladies of contemporary industrial society in terms of the alienation of workers. Through numerous theoretical and empirical research, sociologists have not only put the concept of alienation on a
scientific footing but have also given it a central place in contemporary
social science (Nisbet 1953). The richness of sociological literature
on alienation can be easily estimated from a casual look at three recent bibliographies (Geyer 1972, 1974; Lystad 1969). The Geyer
bibliography of 1972 contains 1,189 entries. A later supplement by
Geyer in 1974 added another 636 entries. The Lystad bibliography
of 1969 contains 225 annotated references. It would not be possible
to adequately review such an enormous amount of material in the sociological literature in a single chapter. However, in the following
pages, some major trends in the sociological literature will be outlined.

Historically speaking, Rousseau was the first person to provide
a sociological treatment of the concept of alienation. Later, Marx
put the concept on firmer analytic ground by providing a link between
the essential nature of workers (realization of individuality) and their
labor. Worker alienation, according to Marx, results when one's
labor does not lead to the realization of one's individuality. Most sociological writings on the subject of alienation draw their inspiration
from the conceptualization of Marx. While building their theses on

18

Marxian notions, contemporary sociologists differed from Marx in one important respect. Marx took the position that very often workers may not be aware of their state of alienation. For example, individuals who are working under supervision in order to achieve financial security for themselves and their families are by definition alienated, whether they realize it or not. They are alienated, according to Marx, because their labor is not free and autonomous and, hence, does not result in establishing their individuality. Contemporary sociologists, on the other hand, consider work alienation as a conscious psychological state of workers that can be measured empirically by assessing workers' beliefs and attitudes toward work. Besides Marx, the work of two other social philosophers, Weber and Durkheim, has significantly influenced the thinking of contemporary sociologists.

WEBER'S TREATMENT OF ALIENATION

Weber's treatment of the concept of alienation is very similar to that of Marx. As Gerth and Mills (1946) put it, "Marx's emphasis upon the wage worker as being 'separated' from the means of production becomes, in Weber's perspective, merely one special case of a universal trend. The modern soldier is equally 'separated' from the means of violence, the scientist from the means of enquiry, and the civil servant from the means of administration" (p. 50). Thus, Weber treated alienation as a much more widespread social phenomenon than did Marx. With respect to the causes of work alienation, Weber's ideas were similar to those of Marx. Both believed that the individuality or personal worth of workers is determined by their labor and that alienation results from working conditions that deny an expression of individuality. But Weber went a step further in asserting the historical antecedents of work alienation. Study of the Protestant religion convinced Weber (1930) that the ethical system of Protestantism trains individuals to be individualists and to believe in the goodness of work. The principles preached in the Protestant faith, such as "God helps those who help themselves" or "work is its own reward," promoted in people a high degree of individualism and a craving for intrinsic rewards and industriousness. "The job was regarded as a sacred calling, and success at work was evidence that one had been chosen for salvation" (Faunce 1968, p. 22). Such were the beliefs that resulted from Protestant training, and, therefore, Weber argued that the Protestant work ethic is the major source of increased work involvement. For Weber, Protestantism laid the foundation for capitalism by increasing the work involvement of entrepreneurs. But for Marx, Protestantism was an ideological justification for capitalism, and Marx felt the capitalistic economy to be the cause of worker alienation.

Weber's exposure to the "American way of life" (political democracy and economic capitalism) and his study of the Protestant religion convinced him that the spirit of the Protestant work ethic is the key to the realization of man's potentialities to the fullest extent. Gerth and Mills (1946) felt that Weber was impressed by the "grandiose efficiency of a type of man, bred by free associations in which the individual had to prove himself before his equals, where no authoritative commands, but autonomous decisions, good sense, and responsible conduct train for citizenship" (p. 18). Such is the image Weber had of an involved worker. Like Marx, Weber also placed emphasis on the freedom to make one's own decisions, on assuming personal responsibility, and on proving one's worth through achievement at work. Although both Marx and Weber saw loss of individuality as the necessary condition for work alienation, they differed in their views on the role of a capitalist economy in producing alienation at work. The reason for the difference in their views lies in the fact that Marx was looking at the jobs of the rank and file, whereas Weber was looking at the jobs of the capitalist entrepreneurs. Translated into motivational terms, Weber's emphasis on the individuality of the entrepreneurs would imply that if the work setup cannot provide an environment that satisfies the needs of entrepreneurs for individual autonomy, responsibility, and achievement, it will create a state of alienation in them.

DURKHEIM'S CONCEPTS OF ANOMIE AND ALIENATION

Unlike Marx and Weber, who viewed alienation as resulting primarily from a perceived lack of freedom and control at work, Emile Durkheim, the French sociologist, saw it as the consequence of a condition of anomie, or the perceived lack of socially approved means and norms to guide one's behavior for the purpose of achieving culturally prescribed goals (Blauner 1964; Durkheim 1893; Shepard 1971). Robert Merton (1957), who made the concept of anomie more popular in contemporary sociology, defined it as "a breakdown in the social structure, occurring particularly when there is an acute disjunction between the cultural . . . goals and the socially structured capacities of members of the group to act in accord with them" (p. 162). Thus, alienation as the consequence of a state of anomie exists when people believe that there is a breakdown of societal behavioral norms (a state of normlessness) and that cultural goals are achieved primarily through deviant behavior. It is such beliefs, rather than actual socially deviant behavior, that define the state of alienation among people.

The condition of anomie is often considered a postindustrial phenomenon. As Blauner (1964) observed, industrialization and urbanization of modern society have "destroyed the normative structure of a more traditional society and up-rooted people from the local groups and institutions which had provided stability and security (p. 24). No longer able to feel a sense of security and belonging, modern men and women find themselves isolated from others. This form of social alienation often results in normlessness and in its collective form manifests itself in various types of urban unrest. In social-psychological terms, this variant of alienation seems to stem from the frustration of social and security needs, the need to belong to groups for social approval and social comparison (Festinger 1954; Maslow 1954). The social-psychological processes that explain how this form of alienation comes about are discussed later in the chapter.

CONTEMPORARY SOCIOLOGICAL TREATMENT OF ALIENATION

The strong impact of Marx, Weber, and Durkheim is quite evident in contemporary sociological writings on the subject of alienation and involvement. For instance, Dubin (1956) defined involvement as a central life interest. According to him, a job-involved person is one who considers work to be the most important part of his or her life and engages in it as an end in itself. A job-alienated person, on the other hand, engages in work in a purely instrumental fashion and perceives work as providing financial resources for more important off-the-job activities. Faunce (1959) also considered job involvement as a commitment to a job in which successful performance is regarded as an end in itself, rather than as a means to some other end. For both Dubin and Faunce, the concepts of involvement and alienation are intimately related to the Protestant work ethic, the moral value of work, and personal responsibility, as conceived by Weber. In fact, most contemporary sociologists view work alienation as a form of dissatisfaction or a feeling of disappointment with jobs, occupations, or work in general, which do not provide intrinsic-need satisfaction or opportunities for self-direction and self-expression. For instance, Seeman (1967) considered alienation to result from work that is not intrinsically satisfying and engaging. According to Seeman (1971), "work alienation is something very close to what Marx meant—namely, engagement in work which is not intrinsically rewarding" (p. 136). Likewise, Miller (1967) conceived of alienation in terms of the lack of intrinsic pride or meaning in work. Blauner (1964) followed Marx and Weber very closely by suggesting that "alienation exists when workers are unable to control their immediate work processes, to develop a sense of purpose and function which connects their jobs to the overall organization of production, to belong to integrated industrial communities, and when they fail to become involved in the activity of work as a mode of personal self-expression" (p. 15). The four major dimensions of work alienation conceived by Blauner in the above quotation are lack of personal control over the work process, a a sense of social isolation, meaninglessness (or lack of task significance), and lack of self-expression. Out of the four dimensions, the sense of social isolation is considered by Blauner as the least descriptive of work alienation. According to Blauner, "a worker may be integrated in the plant community and loyal to the company and still fail to achieve a sense of involvement and self-expression in his work activity itself" (p. 28).

Causes and Correlates of Alienation

Sociological literature dealing with the identification of causes and correlates of work alienation can be divided into three broad categories. First, some sociologists (Goldthorpe, Lockwood, Bechhofer, and Platt 1968) have argued that the attitude of alienation from work depends on prior orientations, which workers develop in their cultural, subcultural, or social class settings. Such work orientations or values are learned through primary- and reference-group influences and are brought by workers to the work situations. For example, several studies (Kohn and Schooler 1969; Morse and Weiss 1955; Sykes 1965) have shown social class and occupational differences with respect to values attached to intrinsic and extrinsic work outcomes. The studies have suggested that white-collar workers tend to hold middle-class work values stressing the importance of intrinsic outcomes, such as personal autonomy, achievement, and control in the job. Blue-collar workers, on the other hand, seem to emphasize extrinsic job outcomes, such as pay and security, and consider work as a means to other ends in their lives. The blue-collar workers, therefore, have been considered by the researchers as being more alienated than the white-collar workers. Such differences were explained by Kohn and Schooler (1969) in terms of social-structural factors. According to Kohn and Schooler, "Conditions of occupational life at higher social class levels facilitate interest in the intrinsic qualities of the job, foster a view of self and society that is conducive to believing in the possibilities of rational action toward purposive goals, and promote self-direction. The conditions of occupational life at lower social class levels limit man's view of the job primarily to the extrinsic benefits it provides (and) foster a narrowly circumscribed conception of self and society" (p. 677). It is the social structure and reference-group influence that determine workers' general outlook and expectations toward the degree of work involvement or alienation.

The second category of explanation advanced by sociologists is in terms of the nature of technology and social organization used at work. For instance, Blauner (1964) argues that worker alienation results from segmented workflow, repetitive jobs carried out at a constant pace, and mechanical control of work operations. All these technological features at work frustrate intrinsic needs of workers, satisfaction of which is essential for worker involvement. In his book, Alienation and Freedom, Blauner compared workers from four different industries: printing, chemical, textile, and automobile. These industries differed in terms of degree of mechanization of technology, division of labor, concentration of economic structure, and bureaucratization of social organization. Blauner reported that workers in the automobile and textile industries were more alienated than workers in the printing and chemical industries. Craft technology of the printing industry and the continuous-process technology of the chemical industry provided the workers with a greater degree of freedom and integration at work than the mechanized assembly-line technology of the automobile industry and the machine-tending technology of the textile industry. Providing a historical perspective to his study, Blauner noted that "in the early period, dominated by craft industry, alienation is at its lowest level and worker's freedom at a maximum. Freedom declines and the curve of alienation . . . rises sharply in the period of machine industry" (p. 182).

Changes in technology within a single industry can also affect worker alienation. Trist and Bamforth (1951) studied the effects of mechanization among British coalminers. Traditionally, the coal-mining operation was carried out in small, cohesive, self-chosen groups. Members of the groups worked in close proximity to one another and experienced strong interpersonal bonds. With the introduction of mechanical coal-cutting and transporting equipment, however, the traditional teams were broken up and were replaced by large shifts of workers distributed over long distances. The change caused a loss of meaning in the work assigned to individual workers. The workers experienced a sense of anomie and isolation resulting in low productivity.

The third category of explanation of work alienation proposed by sociologists is very similar to the social-psychological explanation in terms of frustration of workers' needs and expectations on the job. Etzioni (1968) emphasizes the importance of satisfying the workers' need for control and power on the job to attain greater job involvement. It is quite evident that the three categories of sociological explanations are related. It seems that alienation of workers, according to sociologists, is the result of intrinsic-need dissatisfaction or disconfirmation of expectancies regarding intrinsic work outcomes, which in turn is influenced by social-structural and technological factors.

The thesis that intrinsic-need deprivation owing to social and technological influences is a necessary condition for worker alienation has not gone unchallenged. Several studies in recent years (Hulin 1972; Inkson and Simpson 1975; McKinney, Wernimont, and Galitz 1962) have shown that many workers do not show higher alienation either because they belong to a lower occupational class or because their work is subjected to mechanical control and routinization. In Walker and Guest's study (1952), automobile assembly workers were reported to be showing low levels of aggression, absenteeism, and turnover, often considered expressions of work alienation. Similar results were reported by Goldthorpe and his associates (Goldthorpe 1966; Goldthorpe et al. 1968) in a study of workers employed on the automobile mass-production lines. The study demonstrated that the workers were satisfied with the material rewards they received from their jobs and were not bothered by the repetitive work they had to do. The Vauxhall organization in Luton, England, where the study was conducted, reported low rates of absenteeism and turnover and a very healthy industrial relations record. These findings were interpreted by Goldthorpe as an indication of the workers' contractual and coercive involvement, rather than moral involvement, in work. Goldthorpe's interpretation is obviously influenced by the Marxian distinction between "forced" and "free" labor.

Variants of Alienation

Sociologists have used the term alienation in varied contexts, such as urban alienation and cultural alienation. Such usage of the concept in multiple contexts has given rise to a number of meanings attributed to the concept. In an attempt to integrate the various meanings of the concept in the sociological literature, Seeman (1959, 1971) has proposed five major variants of the concept: powerlessness, meaninglessness, normlessness, isolation, and self-estrangement. According to Seeman, each variant refers to a different, subjectively felt psychological state of the individual caused by different environmental conditions. Several other researchers, particularly Blauner (1964) and Shepard (1971), have used Seeman's classification and have tried to provide operational measures of the different categories of alienation at work. They have also suggested the antecedent physical and social conditions that produce each state of alienation.

Alienation in the form of powerlessness in the most general sense refers to a perceived lack of control over important events that affect one's life. This type of alienation was the primary concern of

Marx while dealing with labor alienation. Seeman (1959), however, provided a social-psychological perspective and defined the sense of powerlessness as "the expectancy or probability held by the individual that his own behavior cannot determine the occurance of the outcomes or reinforcements he seeks" (p. 784). It may be noticed that Seeman's definition of powerlessness resembles Rotter's (1966) conception of people with an external locus of control. Rotter distinguishes two types of people, internal and external, on the basis of their differential learning history. Early socialization experiences condition the externals to perceive themselves as pawns controlled by external forces. Internals, on the other hand, are conditioned to perceive themselves as capable of controlling their own environment. Thus, externals would very much resemble people experiencing the powerlessness variant of alienation. Seeman (1959) recognized this possibility and suggested that "the congruence in these formulations leaves the way open for the development of a closer bond between two languages of analysis—that of learning theory and that of alienation—that have long histories in psychology and sociology" (p. 785).

Although Seeman (1959) conceived of powerlessness to represent an individual's inability to determine the occurrence of any outcome, most sociologists (Levin 1960; Middleton 1963; Neal and Rettig 1963) restrict it to the individual's sense of control over sociopolitical events. Seeman himself used this variant of alienation to explain and describe men's and women's alienation from the larger social order. An individual's inability to control and influence political systems, industrial economies, or international affairs may create a sense of powerlessness. Alienation in the sense of powerlessness has also been observed in job situations. For instance, Shepard (1971) described powerlessness at work as "the perceived lack of freedom and control on the job" (pp. 13-14). Blauner (1964) expressed similar views when he stated that "the non-alienated pole of the powerlessness dimension is freedom and control" (p. 16). According to Blauner, the powerlessness variant of alienation at work results from the mechanization process that controls the pace of work and thus limits workers' free movements. If one analyzes the sociological concept of powerlessness in motivational terms, it becomes obvious that if a situation constantly frustrates an individual's need for autonomy and control, it will create a state of alienation of this type.

The second type of alienation is identified as a cognitive state of meaninglessness in the individual. According to Seeman (1959), a state of meaninglessness exists when "the individual is unclear as to what he ought to believe—when the individual's minimal standards for clarity in decision making are not met" (p. 786). In such a state the individuals are unable to predict social situations and the outcomes

of their own and others' behavior. Other sociologists have characterized the state of meaninglessness as individuals' failure to understand "the very events upon which life and happiness are known to
depend" (Dean 1961, p. 754) or what is going on in the world today
(Middleton 1963). In a sense, the meaninglessness type of alienation
should be characterized in terms of incomprehensibility or inability
to understand one's complex environment. In the work setup, the
meaninglessness variant of alienation may result when workers are
not able to understand the complex system of goals in the organization
and its relation to their own work (Blauner 1964; Shepard 1971).

Meaninglessness can also be viewed in another sense. It may
represent purposelessness or the lack of any goal or goal clarity
(not because of goal complexity, but because of an unstructured goal
or the simple absence of any goal). Thus, in work situations meaninglessness could result from an increasing specialization and division of labor. When the work process is broken down into simple
minuscule tasks, and when such simple tasks involve no real responsibility and decision making, the work situation robs the worker of any
sense of purpose. The job becomes meaningless for the worker.
Translated into motivational terms, this implies that the continued
frustration of an individual's need for assuming personal responsibility and for gaining greater competence on the job (by being more
knowledgeable about the environment for the sake of influencing it)
causes this type of alienation. It may be noted that both the powerlessness and the meaninglessness interpretations of work alienation
bear the mark of the Marxian belief that lack of control and freedom
over the work process is the main cause of alienation.

The two other forms of alienation suggested by Seeman (1959)
have their roots in Durkheim's (1893) description of anomie. Anomie
refers to the perceived conditions of one's social environment, such
as the perception of the breakdown of social norms regulating individual conduct in modern societies. Merton (1957) argued that a state
of anomie exists when institutionally prescribed conducts fail to achieve
culturally prescribed goals. Following Merton, Seeman (1959) defined the anomie situation for an individual as "one in which there is
a high expectancy that socially unapproved behaviors are required to
achieve given goals" (p. 788). The two forms of alienation that result from such perceived conditions of one's social environment are
normlessness and isolation.

Individuals may develop a sense of normlessness when they find
that previously approved social norms are no longer effective in guiding behavior for the attainment of personal goals. In other words,
individuals find that to achieve given goals it is necessary to use socially unapproved behavior. Finding that they can no longer share the
normative system because of its ineffectiveness, the individuals may

develop norms of their own to guide behavior. Because their norms are different from those of others, the individuals may eventually perceive themselves as being separate from society and its normative system. The dissociation of oneself from others results in a perception of social isolation. The dissociation of oneself from social norms results in normlessness or cultural estrangement. Alienation, in the sense of social isolation and cultural estrangement, refers to the perceived states of loneliness and rootlessness, respectively (Seeman 1971). It may be noticed that these two variants of alienation are related, because they stem from the same basic condition of anomie.

States of loneliness and rootlessness have also been identified in work environments. Blauner (1964), for instance, suggested that these forms of social alienation may be manifested on the job owing to the lack of social integration of the worker. When an organization does not provide the worker any opportunity for developing a sense of membership or belonging in the social system, the worker is bound to show a sense of isolation from the system and its goals. From a motivational point of view, the two variants of social alienation, isolation and normlessness, seem to be based on two different social needs of the individual. Continuous frustration of the membership or the belonging need of the individual may be the crucial determinant of the isolation form of alienation. The normlessness form of alienation, however, is determined by continuous frustration of another social need, the need to evaluate oneself through social comparison (Festinger 1954).

In the context of social-influence theories, social psychologists (Jones and Gerard 1967) have postulated two major kinds of influences that groups exert on the individual. They are referred to as the normative and the informational social influences. By being a member of the group and by adhering to the group norms, individuals fulfill their need to belong, to love, and to be loved by others. When, however, the group norms are perceived to be too restrictive and in conflict with the individual's personal goals, these norms cease to influence the individual. The group loses its normative influence on the individual. The individual becomes isolated in relation to the group, perceived as one who no longer belongs to the group and no longer is loved by others in the group. Such a psychological state can be identified as the isolation form of alienation.

Individuals also depend on the group norms for self-evaluation and for evaluating their abilities and opinions (Festinger 1954). Group norms generally provide people with information on how to behave, (what is right and what is wrong). When individuals find that group norms do not provide useful information for self-evaluation, they may separate themselves from these norms and experience a state of normlessness. Thus, in terms of social-influence theory, the two variants of social alienation result from the failure of the groups to exercise the two forms of social influence, normative and informational.

The final variant of alienation proposed by sociologists is self-estrangement. In many ways the characterization of this category of alienation has posed problems for sociological thinkers. Seeman (1971) admits that it is an "elusive idea" (p. 136), but then goes on to operationalize it. According to Seeman, a person is self-estranged when engaged in an activity that is not rewarding in itself but is instrumental in satisfying extrinsic needs, such as the need for money and security. Following Seeman, Shepard (1971) considers instrumental work orientation, (the degree to which one works for extrinsic-need satisfaction) to be an index of the self-estrangement kind of alienation in the work setup. Blauner (1964) suggests that a job encourages self-estrangement if it does not provide the opportunity for expressing "unique abilities, potentialities, or personality of the worker" (p. 26). In motivational terms, Blauner's observation means that whenever workers find their environment (job or work) lacking in opportunities for the satisfaction of self-actualization needs (Maslow 1954) through the expression of their potentialities, they experience a state of self-estrangement. Following Marx, many contemporary sociologists believe that self-estrangement is the heart of the alienation concept, as if all other forms of alienation eventually result in self-estrangement. Blauner (1964) attests to this belief when he says, "When work activity does not permit control (powerlessness), evoke a sense of purpose (meaninglessness), or encourage larger identification (isolation), employment becomes simply a means to the end of making a living" (p. 3). Faunce (1968) also considers self-estrangement to be the final form of alienation in a causal chain. According to Faunce, the powerlessness, meaninglessness, and normlessness variants of alienation are predisposing conditions for both social and self-estrangement. In his words, "The worker who feels powerless and who sees the work place as meaningless and normless is unlikely to be very concerned with the goals of the work organization and is therefore isolated or alienated from it. . . . A person who is isolated . . . in any social situation is necessarily self-estranged in that situation" (p. 90).

CHARACTERISTICS OF THE
SOCIOLOGICAL APPROACH

At this point it may be helpful to identify some dominant considerations that have guided most sociological treatments of the concept of work alienation. First, one notices a stronger emphasis in sociological writings on the analysis and measurement of the state of worker alienation than on the analysis and measurement of the state of worker involvement. In a sense, sociologists have focused their attention on the negative side of the issue, with a clinical perspective on work organizations. Thus, they have been more concerned with the diagnosis of worker alienation in organizations and consequent organizational maladies than with the identification of conditions for work involvement and organizational growth. Like Freudian psychologists who attempt to explain human nature through an analysis of pathological psychological states, sociologists, taking the lead from Marx, have emphasized the analysis of labor alienation and resulting pathological states to explain the nature of sociotechnical systems. In the same way as the Freudian influence in psychology delayed the formulation of growth theories of personality and motivation (Allport 1961; Maslow 1954), the Marxian influence in sociology may have retarded the progress of sociological theories in better understanding the nature of healthy and growing social systems. As is discussed later, unlike the sociological approaches outlined above, the current psychological approaches to the issue are trying to attack the problem from the positive side through the study of the conditions of work involvement.

The second consideration that has dominated various sociological treatments of alienation is their emphasis on studying work alienation in groups and social systems. The level of analysis of the concept in most sociological approaches has been at the social-system level rather than at the individual level. This has created measurement problems. Although sociologists often talk of the frequency of worker hostility and volatile activism, of absenteeism and turnover, of crime rates, and so on as indexes of alienation in work organizations, they find it hard to establish and theoretically justify the validity and the reliability of these measures. The records on such organizational maladies are notoriously unreliable. Very often incidents of activism, crime, and absenteeism go unreported. Even if the incidents are recorded accurately, it is often difficult to infer from these data the state of alienation in individual workers. For instance, an activist employee desiring to bring about changes in the organization may be showing signs of greater involvement in the work environment than would an apathetic, conformist employee.

Third, sociological approaches generally describe the state of work alienation not in specific behavioral terms, but in terms of epiphenomenal categories. As Johnson (1973a) pointed out, alienation is seen as "an epiphenomenal abstraction, collectively summarizing a series of specific behaviors and categorizing them as 'loneliness,' 'normlessness,' 'isolation,' etc." (p. 40). Such epiphenomenal descriptions of the concept may have the flavor of intellectual romanticism, but they have very little scientific value because they pose problems of empirical verification. Different sociologists have used the same epiphenomenal category to describe different psychological and physical conditions. As Schacht (1970) pointed out, the "powerlessness" variant of alienation has been used in many ways, such as the feeling of powerlessness and reactions to the feeling of powerlessness. The concept of alienation as an epiphenomenal abstraction tends to carry excess meaning and, therefore, eludes precise measurement. Besides, such an abstraction merely describes worker alienation; it does not explain it.

Finally, most sociological approaches consider the presence of individual autonomy, control, and power over the work environment as basic preconditions for removing the state of alienation at work. Work alienation involves engaging in work activities that are not intrinsically rewarding in themselves. Work alienation in contemporary sociological literature is measured only by determining the presence or absence of intrinsic factors (autonomy, responsibility, and so on) on the job. Extrinsic job factors are totally excluded from such measures. For instance, Seeman (1971) uses an index of work alienation that consists of

> seven items which ask, in a variety of ways, whether the individual's job is engaging and rewarding in itself —for example, Does the respondent find the job too simple to bring out his best abilities? Does the job really provide a chance to try out one's own ideas? Are there opportunities to make independent decisions, or is it pretty routine work? All of this tells nothing, of course, about other potential satisfactions (all extrinsic) like pay, promotions, fringe benefits, security of employment, working conditions, and the social rewards on the job (which is why work alienation and job satisfaction are not the same thing). [P. 136]

Notice that Seeman distinguishes job satisfaction from work involvement on the basis of whether the worker is satisfied with extrinsic job factors, as opposed to intrinsic job factors. This is reminiscent of the Marxian distinction between "imposed forced labor" and "free self-directed labor."

4

THE PSYCHOLOGICAL
APPROACH

Life without estrangement is scarcely worth living;
what matters is to increase men's capacity to cope
with alienation.

Walter Kaufmann, 1970

A review of the psychological literature on work alienation reveals that the interest in the scientific study of the phenomenon among
psychologists is very recent. Only during the last two decades have
psychologists interested in organizational behavior developed a serious
concern for the study of the phenomena of work alienation and involvement. Thus, the treatment of the concepts of work alienation and involvement in the psychological literature does not have as long and as
rich a tradition as the sociological literature described in the previous
chapter. However, research during the last two decades provides
ample evidence of an upsurge of interest in the phenomena among
psychologists. An increasing popularity for studies on work alienation and involvement has been recorded in a recent literature survey
conducted by Baba (1979). The results of this survey, presented in
Figure 4.1, show an increasing trend of published research on the
topic during the last 15 years.

Although psychological studies on the concepts of alienation and
involvement are on the increase, this has not resulted in any systematic theorizing about the concepts. In a sense, the psychological
approach to the study of alienation and involvement has been of a
more exploratory and empirical nature. Very little attempt has been
made toward development of theories or systematic conceptualization.
In conceptualizing the constructs of alienation and involvement at
work, the psychological literature provides somewhat sketchy descriptions when compared with the sociological approach. Develop-

31

FIGURE 4.1

Interest in the Job-Involvement Construct in Empirical Literature

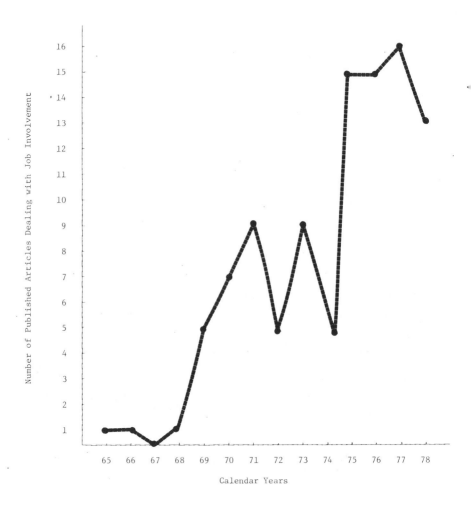

ment of systematic psychological theories that can explain the phenomena of work alienation and involvement and that can have broad
generality across culture are simply absent from the literature.

The sketchy treatment of the subject by psychologists is indicated by the use of many different terms in the psychological literature that describe the psychological states of alienation and involvement at work. Some of the terms listed by Rabinowitz and Hall (1977)
are job involvement, job satisfaction, intrinsic motivation, morale,

ego involvement, occupational involvement, work-role involvement, and central life interests. These terms have been used by different researchers to describe what is thought to be a single construct, and very little effort has been put forth by the researchers (the notable exception being Rabinowitz and Hall 1977) to strive for some conceptual integration.

In the previous chapter it was pointed out that the sociological approach to the study of work alienation emphasizes the analysis and measurement of the state of alienation from work rather than of the state of involvement at work. In contrast to the sociological approach, psychologists have attempted to analyze the problem of alienation from the point of view of job involvement and have attempted to define and measure involvement at work rather than alienation at work. In a sense the two approaches to alienation—the sociological and the psychological—are not as far apart as is commonly believed, but are in fact dealing with two poles of the same continuum.

In trying to explain the nature of job involvement, psychological studies have attempted to answer four major questions. The questions are: What is job involvement? How does it originate? What factors are associated with it and, therefore, can act as its predictors? and What are its effects? The above questions deal, respectively, with the problems of definition of the construct of job involvement, its origin or causes, its correlates, and its effects. The following paragraphs will address these problems.

JOB INVOLVEMENT

The concept of job involvement has been defined in various ways by different psychologists. After an exhaustive review of all definitions of job involvement in psychological literature, Rabinowitz and Hall (1977) concluded that the definitions of job involvement should be grouped into two categories, each representing a distinct way of conceptualizing the construct. One category of definitions views job involvement as a "performance-self-esteem contingency." According to these definitions, job involvement is the extent to which the self-esteem of individuals is affected by their level of performance at work. Thus, higher or lower job involvement means higher or lower self-esteem derived from work behavior. The other category of definitions views job involvement as a "component of self-image." According to this category of definitions, job involvement refers to the degree to which individuals identify psychologically with their jobs.

The idea of viewing job involvement as a performance-self-esteem contingency can be traced back to the work of Allport (1947) on the psychology of participation and ego involvement. Allport suggested that any situation (including the work situation) that "engages the status-seeking motive" (p. 128) of an individual is ego involving. Thus, a person's involvement at work can be viewed as the degree of perceived opportunity at work for status or self-esteem need satisfaction. In the same vein, other researchers (French and Kahn 1962; Gurin, Veroff, and Feld 1960; Vroom 1962) have also considered job involvement as the degree to which performance affects one's self-esteem. For instance, according to Vroom (1962), job involvement exists when good performance enhances one's self-esteem.

The second definition, which views job involvement as a psychological identification with one's job, dates back to the etymological treatment of the concepts of alienation and involvement. However, this definition was first proposed by Lodahl and Kejner (1965) and later adapted by Lawler and Hall (1970). According to Lawler and Hall (1970), job involvement refers to "psychological identification with one's work" or "the degree to which the job situation is central to the person or his identity" (pp. 310-11). Several other researchers have also viewed job involvement in this manner. Patchen (1970) has used the concept of "identification with one's occupation," which is very similar to psychological identification with one's work. Likewise, Maurer (1969) considered work involvement as the degree to which an individual's work role is important in itself and forms the basis of self-definition.

The two distinct conceptual ways of describing job involvement were incorporated into a single questionnaire measure of job involvement by Lodahl and Kejner (1965). According to Lodahl and Kejner, job involvement can be defined in two ways. First, it refers to "the degree to which a person's work performance affects his self-esteem" (p. 25). Second, it also refers to "the degree to which a person is identified psychologically with his work, or the importance of work in his total self-image" (p. 24). These two definitions are quite distinct, and yet Lodahl and Kejner combined the two in their questionnaire instrument and made no attempt in their study to show how the two are related. The questionnaire scale developed by Lodahl and Kejner to measure job involvement has been very widely used by psychologists in job-involvement studies. This suggests that most researchers have uncritically accepted the notion of job involvement reflecting both a "performance-self-esteem contingency" and a "component of self-image" without seeing any need to integrate the two components in any meaningful way.

For better conceptual clarity Lawler and Hall (1970) for the first time argued in favor of a distinction among three psychological states of an individual. According to Lawler and Hall, the psychological state of job involvement should be distinguished from intrinsic motivation on the one hand and job satisfaction on the other. The definition of job involvement should be limited to the notion of psychological identification with one's work or the importance of the total work situation in one's life. Intrinsic motivation, however, should refer to a state of the individual in which satisfaction of intrinsic needs (for example, self-esteem) is contingent upon appropriate job behavior. This description of intrinsic motivation on the job is similar to the performance-self-esteem contingency formulation of job involvement. Thus, Lawler and Hall suggested that the performance-self-esteem contingency at work should be viewed as an index of intrinsic motivation rather than of job involvement. According to these researchers, a state of job satisfaction that is different from both job involvement and intrinsic motivation results from a satisfaction of the needs of the individual through the attainment of job outcomes or rewards without any regard to performance-outcome contingencies.

In another review of the psychological literature on job involvement, Saleh and Hosek (1976) have identified four different interpretations of the concept of job involvement. "A person is involved (1) when work to him is a central life interest; (2) when he actively participates in his job; (3) when he perceives performance as central to his self-esteem; (4) when he perceives performance as consistent with his self-concept" (p. 215). The first interpretation of the concept of involvement in terms of a central life interest (Dubin 1956) is very similar to the interpretation offered by Lawler and Hall (1970). The main idea underlying this interpretation is that the psychological state of involvement with respect to an environment entity (such as a job or family) is a cognitive or perceived state of identification with that entity. The second interpretation of involvement in terms of participation suggests that the psychological state of involvement be viewed as behavioral acts of the individual directed toward the satisfaction of his or her needs for autonomy and control. Bass (1965), for instance, considered participative job behaviors, such as making important job decisions or setting one's own work pace, to be important indexes of greater work involvement. Likewise, Wickert (1951) stressed the opportunity to make job decisions and a feeling of contribution to the achievement of organizational goals to be the main components of job involvement. More recently, SleeSmith (1973) suggested that the essential components of job involvement are cooperation and commitment, finding significance and achievement at work, and treating work as an outlet for one's energy and skill. Other researchers, such as Wiener and Gechman (1977) equated job involvement with work commitment behaviors and defined work commitment behaviors as "socially accepted behaviors that exceed formal and/or normative expectations relevant to the object of commitment" (p. 48). The remaining two interpretations of involvement, namely providing a sense of personal worth (Siegel 1969) and reinforcing one's self-concept

(Vroom 1964), suggest that involvement may be viewed as the experience of satisfaction resulting from the fulfillment of the individual's self-esteem and self-actualization needs. From the results of their own factor analysis, Saleh and Hosek (1976) concluded that job involvement is "the degree to which the person identifies with the job, actively participates in it, and considers his performance important to his self-worth. It is, therefore, a complex concept based on cognition, action, and feeling" (p. 223). It is interesting to note that to achieve conceptual clarity Lawler and Hall (1970) tried to differentiate the state of involvement from intrinsic motivation and job satisfaction, whereas Saleh and Hosek (1976) brought them all together again.

The review of definitions of job involvement clearly suggests a lack of consensus among researchers regarding what the precise meaning of the construct should be. The construct has been defined differently by different researchers. For some it means a form of psychological identification, and for others it is a performance-self-esteem contingency. Some have combined the above two meanings to represent the construct. Furthermore, the construct has also been viewed as a form of cognitive belief, as behavioral tendencies, as an affective state, or a combination of all three. If researchers in this area hold such different views of job involvement, they can neither meaningfully communicate with one another nor build upon each other's work. Consequently, research progress in the area will be retarded. Without an adequate and commonly accepted definition of the construct, future research efforts can only add more confusion to our understanding of the concepts.

CAUSES OF JOB INVOLVEMENT

The definitions of job involvement described in the previous section tend to be influenced by the researchers' notions about the causes of job involvement. This is particularly true for the performance-self-esteem contingency conceptualization of job involvement. Researchers who have defined job involvement as a form of the performance-self-esteem contingency argue that intrinsic-need satisfaction is a necessary condition for job involvement.

In trying to explain the nature of job involvement, psychologists in general have concentrated on the analysis of specific motivation states of the individual in work situations. Psychological explanations are based on motivation theories and, therefore, tend to emphasize the need-satisfying qualities of the job as basic determinants of job involvement. For instance, Vroom (1962) proposed that a person's attempts to satisfy the need for self-esteem through work on the job leads to job involvement. In his study "the degree of job involvement for a particular person was measured by his choice of 'ego' rather than extrinsic factors in describing the sources of satisfaction and dissatisfaction on the job" (p. 161). Vroom seems to emphasize intrinsic-need satisfaction as the essential condition for higher job involvement. In his view, higher autonomy extended to the individual results in higher ego involvement, which in turn leads to a higher level of job performance.

Bass (1965) has echoed similar sentiments by pointing out that involvement in one's job is determined by the presence of six conditions. The conditions are a greater opportunity for making job decisions, the feeling that one is making important contributions to organizational success, an experience of personal success, personal achievement, self-determination, and personal autonomy in matters of setting one's own work pace.

Patchen (1970) identified three general conditions for job involvement. According to him, "Where people are highly motivated, where they feel a sense of solidarity with the enterprise, and where they get a sense of pride for their work, we may speak of them as highly 'involved' in their job" (p. 7). When Patchen talks of workers being highly motivated, he refers to their high levels of achievement need or to their wish to accomplish worthwhile things on the job. When he talks of workers' solidarity with the enterprise, he refers to their need for belonging to the organization. Finally, when he talks of workers' sense of pride, he refers to workers' feeling of high self-esteem. Thus, in Patchen's view, when a job provides opportunities for the satisfaction of one's achievement needs, belonging needs, and self-esteem needs, one experiences a greater degree of job involvement.

Advocates of participative management (Argyris 1964; Likert 1961; McGregor 1960; Walton 1972) have stressed the fact that job involvement results from an organizational (and job) environment designed to promote ego and growth need (Alderfer 1972; Maslow 1954) satisfaction. Likert (1961), for instance, suggested that involvement in one's job results from a supportive psychological climate in an organization that provides a sense of human dignity or satisfies the need for self-esteem. Following the humanistic tradition, both Argyris (1964) and McGregor (1960) explicitly advocated growth theories of human personality and motivation. Both of them suggested that work alienation is the inevitable result of organizational constraints that frustrate natural tendencies of individuals to grow through the satisfaction of intrinsic needs. According to McGregor (1960), the major organizational constraint responsible for employee alienation stems from managerial assumptions about human nature. If the management assumes that people have an inherent dislike for work, avoid responsi-

bility, and seek money and security with as little effort as they can,
it creates conditions within the organization to alienate employees.
McGregor refers to these assumptions as Theory X. But instead of
Theory X, the management can work under a different set of assumptions called Theory Y. Theory Y assumes that people like to work
and want more responsibility, autonomy, and self-control on the job.
Management under Theory Y assumptions can create organizational
conditions, such as participative management, that will reduce worker
alienation or increase worker involvement.

Worker alienation, according to Argyris (1964), is caused by the
properties of formal organization, such as work specialization, strict
chain of command, or span of control. These properties stand in the
way of workers' growth toward psychological maturity and better mental health. Such growth toward maturity involves assuming greater
self-control by becoming more active and independent. When the
growth process is retarded by the properties of the formal organization,
the worker may become either psychologically ill or alienated from
work. Conditions for reducing alienation or increasing involvement,
therefore, must lie in redesigning the organizational and work setup to
promote self-control, self-esteem, and autonomy for the workers.

In contrast to proponents of the performance-self-esteem conceptualization, researchers who are in favor of defining job involvement as a central component of self-image consider job involvement
to be caused by early socialization of the individual. However, they
still maintain that intrinsic-need satisfaction is an important precondition for job involvement. For instance, Lodahl and Kejner (1965),
who defined job involvement as "the degree to which a person is identified psychologically with his work" (p. 24), suggested that such a
psychological state of identification with work may result partly from
early socialization training, during which the individual may inter-
nalize the value of the goodness of work. They stated that the concept
of job involvement "operationalizes the 'protestant ethic' and because
it is a result of the introjection of certain values about work into the
self, it is probably resistant to changes in the person due to the nature of a particular job" (p. 25). However, these researchers also
considered job involvement to represent the degree to which one's
self-esteem is affected by job performance, suggesting that intrinsic-
need satisfaction at work is also important for job involvement to develop.

Lawler and Hall (1970) are also in favor of defining job involvement as the psychological identification with work. They believe that
job involvement is partly caused by an individual's personal background and situations. Still, they maintain that a job-involved person is "one who is affected very much personally by his whole job
situation, presumably because he perceives his job as an important

part of his self-concept and perhaps as a place to satisfy his important needs (e.g., his need for self-esteem)" (pp. 310-11). It appears that in defining the concept of involvement, Lawler and Hall assumed that intrinsic or growth needs (Alderfer 1972) are central to the self-concept of the individual. To emphasize the centrality of intrinsic needs, they pointed out that "the more the job is seen to allow the holder to influence what does on, to be creative, and to use his skills and abilities, the more involved he will be in the job" (p. 310). In the same article, Lawler and Hall (1970) reiterated their position with the following remark: "Other things being equal, more people will become involved in a job that allows them control and a chance to use their abilities than will become involved in jobs that are lacking these characteristics" (p. 311).

Maurer (1969), who considers involvement in terms of work-role motivation, suggests that the centrality of the work role in one's self-image results primarily from "self-evaluation" and "success definition." Self-evaluation is described by Maurer as "the extent to which an individual evaluates or ranks himself as a person in terms of his work role" (p. 26). Success definition is defined as "the degree to which an individual defines success in terms of work role success" (p. 26). Thus, Maurer considers self-esteem and achievement-need satisfaction at work to be the necessary conditions for job involvement.

Blood and Hulin (1967) have viewed job involvement in terms of "integration with middle-class norms." They have proposed that "conditions fostering integration with middle-class norms will also foster adherence to the protestant ethic since the latter is an aspect of the former" (p. 285). Blood and Hulin (1967) have postulated a continuum ranging from integration to alienation with middle-class norms. At the integrated end of the continuum individuals show the maximum amount of personal involvement with their jobs, presumably because of ego-need gratification on the job. At the alienated end of the continuum, the job is seen as a provider of means for "pursuing extra-occupational goals. The concern of these workers is not for increased responsibility, higher status, or more autonomy. They want money, and they want it in return for a minimal amount of personal involvement" (p. 285). In this formulation (see also Hulin and Blood 1968) job involvement is the result of intrinsic-need satisfaction on the job. However, whether or not a worker is alienated from or integrated with middle-class norms (for example, seeking higher responsibility and autonomy on the job) is determined by the nature of the worker's background and environment in which socialization occurs. The authors argue that an industrialized, urban, blue-collar environment is more conducive to producing alienation than a nonindustrial, rural environment.

Following Blood and Hulin's suggestion regarding the environmental determinants of job involvement, Wanous (1974) provides a developmental view of job involvement. According to Wanous, "One of the earliest determinants of an individual's work needs is the environment of his socialization. In the context of a rural or urban white-collar environment, an individual may be more likely to adopt a set of work values similar to what has been called the Protestant work ethic or middle-class work values. As a result of such an upbringing, an individual could develop a general value orientation toward work which emphasizes the importance of work in one's total self-esteem and reinforces the belief that work can hold intrinsic satisfaction" (p. 621). Consideration of intrinsic-need satisfaction on the job as a necessary condition for job involvement led Wanous to speculate that Protestant-work-ethic-oriented individuals will become job involved when the job provides autonomy, variety, challenge, feedback, and task identity. All these job characteristics aim at providing for the satisfaction of intrinsic needs.

The above review of the causes of job involvement shows that almost all researchers consider intrinsic-need satisfaction as the necessary condition for job involvement. Since the satisfaction of intrinsic needs of workers can be achieved only through appropriate changes in the job and the organizational environment, such changes (for example, job variety, autonomy, opportunity for participation) have also been viewed as situational factors causing job involvement (Rabinowitz and Hall 1977). Besides the situational variables at the work place that affect intrinsic motivation, researchers have also identified the Protestant-work-ethic attitude as a possible cause of job involvement. The Protestant-work-ethic attitude is largely determined by past socialization processes experienced by individuals in specific socioeconomic and cultural milieu in which they have lived. Thus, the rural/urban, blue-collar/white-collar, and ethnocultural backgrounds of individuals have been considered as causes of job involvement. Since the Protestant-work-ethic attitude is a product of past socialization processes of individuals, it is believed to be a more stable predisposition than the intrinsic needs. Thus, Rabinowitz and Hall (1977) consider the Protestant-work-ethic attitude as a personal factor or individual-difference variable causing job involvement.

The categorization of factors causing job involvement into situational and individual-difference variables seems theoretically unsound. Rather, a classification in terms of predisposing and precipitating factors of job involvement is more appropriate. If one closely examines what Rabinowitz and Hall (1977) lable as situational variables causing job involvement, one may find the following causal sequence: presence and activation of intrinsic needs in the individual at work ➞ work behavior ➞ presence of certain job or organizational-outcome variables such as job autonomy, job variety, participative organizational climate, and so on → perceived potential of the job to satisfy the intrinsic needs → job involvement. In this case the causes of job involvement include both situational variables, such as job and organizational characteristics, and personal variables, such as the strength of intrinsic needs of the individual. If one considers the other category of causes referred to by Rabinowitz and Hall (1977) as individual-difference variables, one will find the following sequence: socioeconomic and cultural environment that has influenced the individual in the past → internalization of Protestant-work-ethic values → presence and activation of intrinsic needs at work → work behavior → presence of certain job and organizational outcomes → perceived job potential to satisfy the intrinsic needs → job involvement. Here again, the causes of job involvement include both situational variables, such as sociocultural environment (rural/urban background, ethnocultural environment, and so on) responsible for individual past socialization, and individual-difference variables, such as work values of the individual. However, one can easily distinguish two sets of predisposing and precipitating factors in the causal chain. The situational variables responsible for an individual's past socialization and the individual variable of internalized work values are clearly predisposing causal factors of job involvement. The precipitating causal factors of job involvement would include the situational variables, such as the job or the organizational outcomes, and the individual variable of intrinsic-need strength.

CORRELATES OF JOB INVOLVEMENT

Psychological theories of job alienation and involvement have not made a clear distinction among the causes, effects, and other correlates of the phenomena. Most researchers have found it difficult to make such a distinction, because most of the empirical studies interested in discovering the antecedent or consequent conditions of job involvement are of correlational nature. While the correlational studies (particularly those using the path-analytic approach) have aided in making causal inferences about the phenomena and their effects, one must exercise extreme caution interpreting these inferences. From a theoretical and methodological standpoint, it is important to make the distinction between the causes, effects, and correlates of job involvement. All causal factors discussed in the previous section are also correlates of job involvement, but the causal factors are conceived as necessary and sufficient antecedent conditions. Their presence necessarily leads to the presence of a state of job involvement in the individual. For example, if the strength of intrinsic needs and the perceived potential of a job to satisfy these intrinsic needs are considered as causal variables, one would expect that they would correlate or covary with job involvement. However, there are other correlates that are not causal variables. For example, personal variables, such as age or education, and situational variables, such as salary or job level, may correlate with job involvement but cannot be considered as direct causes of job involvement.

Furthermore, job behavior or job attitudes, such as absenteeism or job satisfaction, that are affected by job involvement have also been treated by the researchers as correlates of job involvement. But these variables are effects or necessary consequent conditions of job involvement and, therefore, should be distinguished from other correlates of job involvement, such as age or education of the worker. The nature and strength of the association between a correlate, such as age and job involvement, tend to be mediated by many factors besides the causes or effects of job involvement. For instance, the observation that age is positively related to job involvement has been partly explained by the fact that older employees experienced the Great Depression and, as a result, came to value work more in their lives (Cherrington 1977).

The reason for exploring the nature of the correlates that are neither direct causes nor direct effects of job involvement are three-fold. First, knowing what factors do or do not covary with job involvement provides the researcher with an understanding of the phenomenon at a descriptive level. On the basis of the correlates, one can describe what a job-involved person looks like. Rabinowitz and Hall (1977) have provided such a description when they state "the job-involved person is a believer in the Protestant Ethic, is older, has internal (vs. external) locus of control, has strong growth needs, has a stimulating job (high autonomy, variety, task identity, and feedback), participates in decisions affecting her or him, is satisfied with the job, has a history of success, and is less likely to leave the organization" (p. 284). Such a description, however, does not provide a precise and direct explanation of the phenomenon or what factors cause job involvement in a person. Causal variables have explanatory properties, whereas other correlates have only descriptive properties.

Second, knowing how much variables correlate with job involvement helps the researcher to use those variables as predictors of job involvement. If one knows that age or level of education strongly covaries with job involvement, they can be used as predictors of job involvement in organizational contexts. As predictors, such variables are easy, economical, and less time-consuming to measure.

The third reason for studying the correlates of job involvement is simply to discover why some factors covary with job involvement and others do not. What are the reasons underlying the presence or absence of covariation? Such discovery helps our understanding of the complex nature of job involvement.

TABLE 4.1

Correlates of Job Involvement

Personal Variables		Situational Variables		
Demographic	Psychological	Job	Organization	Sociocultural Environment
Age	Intrinsic/extrinsic-need strength	Job characteristics/outcomes	Organization climate (participative/mechanistic)	Size of community
Education	Work values	Variety	Organization size (large/small)	Rural/urban
Sex	Locus of control	Autonomy	Organization structure (tall/flat)	Ethnic culture
Marital status	Satisfaction with job characteristics/outcomes	Task identity	Organization control system (precise/vague)	Religion
Occupation	Job effort	Feedback		
Seniority	Job performance	Job level (formal status in organization)		
	Absenteeism	Salary level		
	Turnover potential	Working conditions		
		Job security		
		Supervision		
		Interpersonal climate		

From a methodological standpoint, investigation of more direct and immediate causes and effects of job involvement should use a different research strategy than those used for other correlates, such as age or education. Both the experimental or quasi-experimental designs (Cook and Campbell 1976) and the longitudinal approach seem more appropriate in the former case, whereas the multivariate and correlational designs (Weiss 1976) are more appropriate in the latter case.

The correlates of job involvement in the psychological literature have been classified in terms of whether they are personal characteristics, situational characteristics, or work outcomes. Such a descriptive classification is based on the theoretical perspective that job involvement is determined by both personal and situational factors (Rabinowitz and Hall 1977) and that it has effects on job attitudes and behavior. What Rabinowitz and Hall and Saal (1978) have treated as work outcome variables (such as job satisfaction) are, in fact, effect variables. Since these effects are identified in workers' attitudes and behavior, they can be treated as a part of the personal variable category. A simple categorization scheme for all the correlates is presented in Table 4.1. It must be emphasized that the categorization is purely a descriptive classification of factors that may or may not correlate with job involvement.

The various factors listed in Table 4.1 under personal and situational categories are by no means exhaustive, but they are drawn from the existing psychological literature. The personal factors are further subdivided into personal demographic factors and personal psychological factors. Such a division has been proposed by Saal (1978) on the basis of his multivariate analysis of several personal and situational correlates of job involvement. Saal suggests that personal psychological variables share a more common variance with job involvement than personal demographic variables. The situational factors are subdivided into three groups: those that are job characteristics, those that are organizational characteristics, and those that are the characteristics of the past and present sociocultural milieu influencing the individual. The following is a brief description of the extent to which these variables are related to job involvement.

Personal Variables

Age

Some researchers have argued that older workers should show greater work involvement than younger workers. Cherrington (1977) has advanced three possible reasons for the positive relationship between age and work involvement. First, with increasing age, a worker is bound to get exposed to greater numbers and different kinds of work experiences. These experiences may form the basis of work involvement. Second, older workers have had specific historical experiences, such as the Great Depression or World War II. These early experiences may have strengthened their work values. Finally, the younger workers of today's affluent society receive training and socialization pressures that make work less important in their lives. Hence, the younger workers show less work involvement. These reasons, however, are not compelling enough to suggest that work involvement will always covary with age. Increasing work experiences with jobs that constantly frustrate individual needs may, in fact, lead to greater work alienation (Argyris 1964). Past socialization experiences and the training of workers vary from culture to culture and from country to country. Hence, what may be true of U.S. workers may not be true for workers in other parts of the world.

The empirical evidence on the relationship between age and work involvement is both weak and conflicting (Rabinowitz and Hall 1977). An examination of 23 studies reveals that 12 studies reported a positive relationship (Aldag and Brief 1975; Cherrington, Condie, and England 1979; Hall and Mansfield 1975; Jones, James, and Bruni 1975; Koch and Steers 1978; McKelvey and Sekaran 1977; Newman 1975; Rabinowitz, Hall, and Goodale 1977; Saal 1978; Schwyhart and Smith 1972; Steers 1975; Susman 1973); eight studies reported no relationship (Bigoness 1978; Gechman and Wiener 1975; Gurin, Veroff, and Feld 1960; Ivancevich and McMahon 1977; Lodahl and Kejner 1965; Mannheim 1975; Mitchell, Baba, and Epps 1975; Torbert and Rogers 1973; and two studies reported a negative relationship (Lefkowitz 1974; Taylor and Thompson 1976).

The findings of many of the above studies have been based on bivariate analysis, and the average magnitude of relationship between age and job involvement is 0.25 as reported by Rabinowitz and Hall (1977). However, the bivariate relationship does not reveal the true picture. Since age is also related to other variables, such as level of education or seniority in a job, a simple correlation between age and job involvement without simultaneously considering the contribution of other related variables does not provide a true picture of the relationship. Furthermore, the mixed results reported by these studies could stem from two major sources: differences in methods used in these studies to collect data on job involvement and differences in the nature of the relationship between age and job involvement among various subsets of respondents, such as more successful and less successful workers (Rabinowitz and Hall 1977) or engineers and nurses (Lodahl and Kejner 1965). In order to have a better understanding of the relationship, one would recommend the use of valid, reliable, and comparable measures of job involvement; more longi-

tudinal than cross-sectional studies; and more multivariate than bivariate analysis of the data.

Education

As in the case of age, the relationship between the levels of
education (or years of education) and job involvement is weak. Rabinowitz and Hall (1977) suggest that the observed low relationship might
be owing to the very restricted range of educational levels studied in
many studies. Empirical evidence on the direction of the relationship
is mixed. Baba (1979) reports that "among the 16 studies investigat-
ing the relationship between education and job involvement, 6 reported
a positive relationship (Cleland, Bass, McHugh, and Montano 1976;
Gadbois 1971; Gurin, Veroff, and Feld 1960; Lefkowitz 1974; Mannheim 1975; Newman 1975); 4 found a negative relationship (Aldag and
Brief 1975; Baba and Jamal 1976; Koch and Steers 1978; Saal 1978);
and 5 showed no relationship (Ivancevich and McMahon 1977; Jones,
James, and Bruni 1975; Rabinowitz, Hall, and Goodale 1977; Ruh,
White, and Wood 1975; Siegel and Ruh 1973). The study by Schuler
(1975) suggested the variables were related but did not report either
the magnitude or direction" (p. 7). Such mixed evidence also goes
with a lack of rationale for expecting levels of education to correlate
with job involvement. Unless one assumes that formal education in
schools and colleges in every society trains one to adopt positive work
values, there is no justification for expecting education to covary with
work involvement. Some studies (Siegel and Ruh 1973) suggest that
education may not covary with job involvement but may moderate the
relationship of job involvement with other correlates, such as participative decision making. For instance, Siegel and Ruh (1973) reported
that workers with a higher level of education showed a stronger par-
ticipation-involvement relationship ($r = .62$) than workers with a lower
level of education ($r = .51$).

Sex

Traditional sex role socialization trains men to believe that they
are the ones who should work, build careers for themselves, and provide economic support for the family. Females, on the other hand,
are trained to accept the role of a housewife. Such beliefs have led
to the expectation that men as a group might show more work involvement than women (Hollon and Gemmill 1976; Koch and Steers 1978;
Newman 1975; Rabinowitz, Hall, and Goodale 1977; Saal 1978). However, the traditional socialization norms are undergoing change, and
the extent to which sex as a variable will continue to covary with work
involvement in the future is suspect. Besides, as Rabinowitz (1975)
has observed, when the effects of other correlates, such as job level

or seniority, are removed, sex differences in job involvement may disappear.

Marital Status

It is difficult to speculate whether a married worker is expected to be more job involved than a worker who is single. On the one hand, married workers have many family obligations that can divert their attention from the job and thereby make them less involved. On the other hand, in order to meet the family obligations, the worker may have to work harder on the job and thereby become more involved. Kanungo, Misra, and Dayal (1975) found married workers to be more involved. However, several other studies (Lodahl and Kejner 1965; Saal 1978) have found no relationship. Comparisons among single workers and married workers coming from single-career and dual-career families need to be made to increase our understanding of how marital status relates to work involvement.

Occupation

Occupational levels of workers, as measured by some socio-economic indexes (for example, Duncan 1961), may be related to job involvement. Ordinarily it is assumed that blue-collar workers are more alienated than white-collar workers, because the former occupations provide a lower satisfaction of intrinsic needs. If this is true, one would also expect clerical workers to be less work involved than managerial workers within the white-collar community. However, there are not many studies that systematically deal with the relationship between occupation and work involvement; thus, such claims remain speculative.

Seniority

The relationship of job or organizational tenure with job involvement has been investigated by several researchers. Baba (1979) cited 15 studies dealing with this issue. Seven of these studies reported a positive relationship (Aldag and Brief 1975; Ivancevich and McMahon 1977; Jones, James, and Bruni 1975; Kanungo, Misra, and Dayal 1975; Newman 1975; Rabinowitz, Hall, and Goodale 1977); one reported a negative relationship (Davis 1966); and seven reported insignificant relationships (Baba and Jamal 1976; Gechman and Weiner 1975; Hall and Mansfield 1975; Mitchell, Baba, and Epps 1975; Saal 1978; Schneider, Hall, and Nygren 1971; Schwyhart and Smith 1972) between seniority and job involvement. It is important to make a distinction between a worker's seniority on the job and seniority in the organization. Most studies in the literature dealing with seniority as a correlate have not paid careful attention to such a distinction. A longer stay within an organization may develop organizational loyalty in a worker, but such loyalty may or may not reflect job involvement. On the other hand, seniority on the job may be more directly related to job involvement than to organizational involvement.

Intrinsic/Extrinsic-Need Strength

On the basis of the importance a person attaches to needs, workers have been classified into two groups: intrinsically and extrinsically motivated workers. Intrinsically motivated workers attach a greater importance to the satisfaction of esteem, achievement, and growth needs (Alderfer 1972; Maslow 1954) at work. Extrinsically motivated workers, on the other hand, attach a greater importance to the satisfaction of social and security needs at work. Since most psychological literature suggests that job involvement is the result of intrinsic-need satisfaction on the job, Lawler (1973) and Hackman and Oldham (1976) have argued that intrinsic-need strength should covary with job involvement. These researchers contend that intrinsically motivated individuals should show higher job involvement than extrinsically motivated individuals when the job meets their respective salient needs.

Empirical research in the area has generally supported this contention (Baba 1979; Rabinowitz and Hall 1977). Baba (1979) reviewed several studies that obtained a positive relationship between growth-need strength and job involvement (Hall, Goodale, Rabinowitz, and Morgan 1978; Hall and Schneider 1972; Hall, Schneider, and Nygren 1970; Kanungo, Misra, and Dayal 1975; Maurer 1969; Rabinowitz, Hall, and Goodale 1977; Saal 1978; Steers 1975; Steers and Braunstein 1976). The strength of the relationship varied considerably from one study to another. However, studies that dealt with the relationship between need for achievement and job involvement (Saal 1978; Steers 1975) showed greater consistency in demonstrating a positive relationship between the two variables.

Although considerable attention has been paid to the relationship between intrinsic-need strength and job involvement, very little research has been done to explore how job involvement is related to extrinsic-need strength. It is quite possible that the need strength of extrinsically motivated workers may relate to job involvement when the job is perceived to have the potential for satisfying these needs. However, researchers have ignored extrinsic needs because of the belief that intrinsic, and not extrinsic, need satisfaction is a necessary condition for job involvement.

Work Values

Lodahl and Kejner (1965) and Bass and Barrett (1972) suggested that job involvement operationalizes Protestant-work-ethic values.

Hence, if a worker strongly believes in Protestant-work-ethic values, that worker would automatically show greater job involvement. Results of studies dealing with this straightforward relationship have been quite ambiguous. Rabinowitz, Hall, and Goodale (1977) and Saal (1978) reported a positive relationship, while Aldag and Brief (1975) reported no significant relationship. Furthermore, Rabinowitz and Hall (1977) reported a wide variation in the magnitude of the relationship. Considering such ambiguity in results, one has to agree with Baba's (1979) suggestion for more research at a conceptual level, defining the constructs before plunging into the discovery of an empirical relationship between the two variables.

Locus of Control

Rotter (1966) developed the notion of locus of control as a stable dimension of personality. Accordingly, he developed an internal-external locus-of-control scale (I-E scale) to distinguish people who are internals from those who are externals. The internals perceive themselves as personally responsible for rewarding and punishing events they experience in their lives, whereas the externals perceive themselves as pawns controlled by external forces. Runyon (1973) argued that internality and job involvement should go hand in hand, because the need to assume personal responsibility for one's own actions (an intrinsic need) plays a central role in both cases. This expectation was confirmed by Kimmons and Greenhaus (1976) and Runyon (1973), who found a positive relationship between job involvement and internal locus of control. However, two other studies (Bigoness 1978; Rabinowitz, Hall, and Goodale 1977) did not find any significant relationship between the two variables.

Several other correlates of job involvement included in the personal variable category (for example, job satisfaction, effort expenditure on the job, workers' job performance, absenteeism) will be discussed later in the section on the effects of job involvement.

Situational Variables

Job Characteristics or Outcomes

From the point of view of job design, it is important to know what characteristics of the job are related to job involvement. Herzberg (1966) has divided job characteristics into two groups: job-content factors and job-context factors. Although job involvement can be related to changes in both sets of factors, most psychological researchers have advocated changes only in the job-content factors. Herzberg proposed job-enrichment programs as a means to increase job involvement, based on the belief that job involvement results from those job changes that satisfy workers' intrinsic needs. Likewise, Hackman and Oldham (1976) identified five core job characteristics (variety, autonomy, task identity, task significance, and feedback) that need to be introduced in a job-enrichment program. It is generally believed that the presence or absence of these job characteristics are associated with job involvement or alienation, respectively. Here again, the emphasis is on those job factors that are mainly responsible for intrinsic-need satisfaction.

Empirical research on job-enrichment programs, however, suggests that job involvement correlates with the five core job factors for workers who have strong intrinsic needs, but not for workers who have weak intrinsic needs. Systematic research on how job involvement may be related to other job characteristics, such as salary and working conditions in both intrinsically and extrinsically motivated workers, is almost nonexistent. However, there are some research studies that have explored the relationship of job involvement with supervision, interpersonal climate, and job level.

Several studies looking at the relationship of job involvement with the nature of supervision have been reported by Rabinowitz and Hall (1977) and Baba (1979). These studies suggest that the nature of supervision is, at best, an equivocal predictor of job involvement. For instance, Brief, Aldag, and Wallden (1976), using the Ohio State Leader Behavior Description Questionnaire (LBDQ) as a measure of supervision, found a positive relationship between job involvement and "initiating structure" behavior of supervisors but did not find any relationship between job involvement and "consideration" behavior of supervisors. Opposite results were reported by Herman, Dunham, and Hulin (1975). Other studies (Dunne, Stahl, and Melhart 1978; Jones, James, and Bruni 1975) reported no significant relationship between supervisory behavior and job involvement.

The lack of agreement among these studies stems from several sources. First, the nature of supervision as a construct is complex, multidimensional, and measured in different ways in different studies. For instance, the LBDQ used by Brief, Aldag, and Wallden (1976) measures supervision in two independent dimensions: initiating structure and consideration. Others (Jones, James, and Bruni 1975) have viewed supervision as representing six different types of behavior, such as support, effectiveness, goal emphasis, or work facilitation. Second, the nature of the relationship between job involvement and supervision is moderated by the nature of the job that is supervised. It is quite natural to expect job involvement to covary with initiating structure and not with consideration among police officers, as Brief, Aldag, and Wallden (1976) found. This may not hold true for other civilian service organizations. Finally, there is no clear reason why supervisory behavior should relate to job involvement. Although the path-goal theory of leadership (House 1971) suggests that high consideration and high structure on the part of the supervisor would facilitate goal attainment of subordinates and, thereby, increase their job involvement, such reasoning appears too simplistic.

The studies on the relationship of job involvement to the interpersonal climate at work suffers from the same type of problems discussed in the previous paragraph. There is neither clarity nor agreement with respect to the nature of the construct "interpersonal climate." The construct has been described and measured in various ways, such as "social factors" (Baba 1979; Rabinowitz and Hall 1977); "group and organizational dynamics" (Alderfer and Lodahl 1971); "friendship opportunities on the job" (Saal 1978); "interpersonal relationships" (Friedlander and Margulies 1969; Herman, Dunham, and Hulin 1975; Newman 1975); "number of people contacted"; "interdependence on the job" (Lodahl and Kejner 1965); "team involvement" (Lodahl 1964); "peer group cohesion" (Buchanan 1974); "supportive climate" (Hall and Hall 1976); and "organizational climate" (Friedlander and Margulies 1969; Jones, James, Bruni, and Sells 1977; Waters, Roach, and Batlis 1974). The results of the various studies show no consistent pattern of relationship, either in terms of direction or magnitude. While one might argue that the interpersonal climate at work fulfills the social needs of the workers and, thereby, may increase their job involvement, "considerable theoretical progress has to be made toward identifying specific factors of importance, before any fruitful outcomes can be expected in the empirical realm" (Baba 1979, p. 15).

Tannenbaum (1966) argued that workers holding higher-level jobs in an organization should show more job involvement than workers holding lower-level jobs. This expectation is based on the assumption that higher-level jobs can satisfy intrinsic needs to a greater extent by offering more variety, autonomy, and challenge to the workers than the lower-level jobs. However, studies performed on this issue provide mixed results. Baba (1979) cited nine studies, of which five found a positive relationship (Chatterjee and Ganguly 1977; Cleland et al. 1976; Davis 1966; Mannheim 1975; Newman 1975); the other four indicated no significant relationship between the two variables (Lodahl and Kejner 1965; Mitchell, Baba, and Epps 1975; Rabinowitz 1975 [cited in Rabinowitz and Hall 1977]; Schuler 1975).

Organizational Variables

Variables included under this section are not necessarily job specific, rather they are organizationwide characteristics. Organizational size, structure, and climate are perceived by the workers as organizational characteristics; nevertheless, they affect worker behavior both on and off the job. For instance, workers belonging to a large organization may feel more alienated at work than workers belonging to a small organization because a large organization tends to frustrate workers' ego needs by being more formal, impersonal, and mechanical in its operation. There are not many studies that report the relationship of job involvement to such organizational variables.

Likert (1961) suggested that a participative organizational climate may increase worker involvement because such a climate contributes toward the fulfillment of intrinsic needs of the worker. Most researchers exploring the relationship of a participative climate in an organization to job involvement have considered it as a job variable or as a characteristic of supervision. As a form of supervisory behavior, participative management style has been found to be positively related to job involvement (Gardell 1977; Ruh, Johnson, and Scontrino 1973; Ruh, White, and Wood 1975; Sakeh and Hosek 1976; Siegel and Ruh 1973; Steers 1976; White 1978; White and Ruh 1973). As an organizational characteristic, participative management has not been directly related to job involvement, although Tannenbaum (1966) and Likert (1961) have argued in favor of a positive relationship. Studies on the relationship of job involvement to organizational size, structure, and control systems are simply nonexistent.

Sociocultural Factors

Variables such as rural/urban background, ethnic-cultural background, and religious background are thought to be related to job involvement. The reason for such a relationship lies in the fact that the socialization process to which these sociocultural factors contribute acts as a predisposing cause of job involvement. The results of the studies exploring the relationship between job involvement and the sociocultural factors are quite ambiguous. For instance, some studies reported a positive relationship between community size (a surrogate for rural/urban background) and job involvement (Ruh, White, and Wood 1975; Siegel and Ruh 1973), whereas other studies reported no significant relationship between the two variables (Saal 1978). No study has been reported that deals with ethnic-cultural and religious backgrounds of workers as correlates.

The above discussion of the correlates of job involvement reveals that our understanding of the relationships is far from adequate. In the case of most variables mixed results have been obtained, primarily because of the inadequate conceptualization and lack of uniform measurement of the constructs. Now we may turn to an examination of the effects of job involvement on the behavior of workers.

EFFECTS OF JOB INVOLVEMENT

Both psychologists and organization theorists have assumed that the attitude of involvement or alienation at work has consequences both for the worker and the organization. It is believed that alienation at work can affect both membership behavior, such as turnover potential and absenteeism of workers, and productive behavior, such as the amount of effort spent on the job and level of performance achieved on the job. In addition, alienation at work can also affect other job attitudes, such as the intensity and quality of psychological satisfaction derived from the various intrinsic and extrinsic job outcomes. The consequences of work alienation on the total organizational effectiveness as indexed by profits or losses, productivity figures, man-hours lost, and so on are mediated by the direct effects of work alienation on workers' job behavior and attitudes.

Empirical research in the psychological literature dealing with the effects of job involvement has mainly concentrated on the relationship of job involvement to five effect variables: satisfaction with job characteristics or outcomes, effort expenditure on the job, performance on the job, absenteeism, and turnover. Although both satisfaction and performance variables are generally treated as effects of job involvement, they can also play a role as causal factors of job involvement. For instance, work alienation can be viewed as a psychological state that results in dissatisfaction among workers toward various job outcomes, as well as nonproductive behavior, such as sabotage and goldbricking. However, alienation can also be viewed as being caused by such dissatisfaction and nonproductive performances in the first place. For instance, satisfaction of the salient needs of workers and feedback from a good performance may increase worker involvement on the job. Like most complex social phenomena, job involvement and its causes and effects are interactive in nature.

Satisfaction with Job Characteristics or Outcomes

A large number of studies have explored the relationship between job satisfaction and job involvement. Overall, these studies have demonstrated a positive relationship between intrinsic-need satisfaction and job involvement (Aldag and Brief 1975; Baba and Jamal 1976; Bigoness 1978; Gannon and Hendrickson 1973; Hall et al. 1978; Herman, Dunham, and Hulin 1975; Hollon and Chesser 1976; Lodahl and Kejner 1965; Mukherjee 1969, 1970; Newman 1975; Rous-

seau 1978; Saal 1978; Schuler 1975; Schwyhart and Smith 1972; Weissenberg and Gruenfeld 1968; Wood 1971). The study by Weissenberg
and Gruenfeld (1968) can be cited as an example. The researchers
investigated the relationship between satisfaction with various job
factors and job involvement. They concluded that increased job involvement is positively related to satisfaction with motivators or job-
content factors (Herzberg 1966), such as achievement, responsibility,
and independence. These motivators tend to satisfy the intrinsic
needs of an individual. Extrinsic needs, however, are satisfied
through job-context factors, such as company policies, nature of supervision, salary, benefits, and working conditions. According to
these researchers, satisfaction with the job-context factors is unrelated to job involvement, but job involvement can be predicted from
satisfaction with the motivators in the job. Although the intrinsic-
need satisfaction and involvement relationship is found to be positive
and quite stable across many studies, there is considerable ambiguity
with respect to the relationship between extrinsic-need satisfaction
and job involvement. In fact there are fewer reported studies that
deal with this issue, and their results are ambigious. For instance,
Gannon and Hendrickson (1973) found that job involvement was positively related to satisfaction with some extrinsic-job outcomes, such
as interpersonal relations and supervision, but was not related to
satisfaction with other extrinsic outcomes, such as pay and promotion.
Schuler (1975), however, reported a positive relationship between job
involvement and satisfaction with each of the four job outcomes: supervision, coworkers, pay, and promotion.

The regularity with which many studies have reported a positive
relationship between job involvement and intrinsic-need satisfaction
(Rabinowitz and Hall 1977) is quite consistent with the positive relationship observed between job involvement and intrinsic-need strength.
However, the research literature is deficient with respect to reported
studies on the relationship of job involvement to extrinsic-need
strength on the one hand and to extrinsic-need satisfaction on the
other.

Effort Expenditure on the Job

It is quite logical to expect that a more job-involved worker
would spend more time and effort working on the job than a less job-
involved worker. A worker who is highly job involved by definition
perceives the job both to be more central to life and to have more potential for salient-need satisfaction. Thus, such a worker will spend
more effort on the job than a worker who is less job involved. Very
few empirical studies have been reported dealing with this issue, and

they provide mixed results. Four recent studies reported positive correlations (Hall and Foster 1977; Hall et al. 1978; Kanungo and Wright 1981; Lawler and Hall 1970); one reported a negative correlation (Cummings and Mauring 1977); and two other studies reported no significant relationship between the two variables (Ivancevich and Mc-Mahon 1977; Schuler 1975). It is difficult to see why empirical results are so mixed when the theoretical rationale for the positive relationship between effort and involvement seems quite sound. It is very likely that in some of the studies the validity of the instruments measuring the constructs (both effort and involvement) is questionable. Perhaps with greater refinement of these measures and with the use of supplementary nonreactive measures (such as percentage of leisure time spent on job-related activities), one would find a more stable positive relationship between effort and job involvement. For instance, in a recent international study of managers from four different countries (Britain, Canada, Japan, and France), Kanungo and Wright (1981) found job involvement to positively covary with the amount of leisure time spent on job activities. Spillover of job activities to leisure time is an indirect, nonreactive measure of effort expenditure that holds future research promise.

Performance

On theoretical grounds, there can be no simple, straightforward relationship between job involvement and performance. Performance of workers is defined by the organization; hence, the level of effort spent by a worker on the job may or may not translate into the level of performance demanded by the organization. The expectancy theory of motivation (Lawler 1973) suggests that the relationship between effort and performance of a worker has to be moderated by several other psychological variables, such as the abilities, training, and role perceptions of the worker. The same variables should also moderate the relationship between job involvement and performance. Thus, the manner in which job involvement affects performance will depend on other worker characteristics, such as past training, ability, and role perceptions. Besides the role of moderating variables, another factor that precludes the possibility of obtaining a simple relationship between job involvement and performance is the multiple performance criteria used by organizations. Sometimes organizations emphasize quality of performance, and at other times they emphasize quantity of performance. Sometimes performance (both quality and quantity) is inadequately measured because of the complexity of job tasks. For these reasons, empirical evidence on the relationship between performance and job involvement has been very confusing.

Several studies have reported a positive, but weak, relationship between job involvement and performance (Hall et al. 1978; Vroom 1962). Vroom, for instance, suggested the relationship is weak because job involvement would increase performance only when the job requires abilities that are valued and possessed by the workers. Steers (1975) likewise reported a positive relationship between job involvement and performance only among those workers who had a high need for achievement. For the workers with a low need for achievement, the relationship was insignificant. In another study, Hall and Lawler (1970) found that job involvement was positively related to only one of three performance measures used. In their study, job involvement of a group of professionals was significantly related to "global technical performance," but not to "objective" or "composite" performance measures. Other researchers (Lawler 1970; Siegel and Ruh 1973) have argued that the quality, rather than quantity, of job performance is more likely to be affected by job involvement.

Some studies have reported simply an absence of any relationship between job involvement and performance (Goodman, Rose, and Furcon 1970; Hall and Foster 1977; Ivancevich and McMahon 1977; Lodahl and Kejner 1965; Saal 1978; Schuler 1975; Siegel and Ruh 1973), perhaps because they failed to include moderator variables and appropriate performance measures in their research designs. It seems that, at the present stage, an understanding of the role of moderator variables is at best incomplete. Added to this, the concepts of both performance and involvement are wrought with considerable ambiguity. Unless the construct validity of performance (Cummings and Schwab 1973) and involvement (Kanungo 1979) are established, empirical studies in this area will continue to yield inconclusive results.

Turnover Potential

It seems quite reasonable to assume that when workers are highly job involved, they would not wish to withdraw from the job and consequently would show less turnover and absentee potential. Empirical research in the area of turnover lends support to the above contention (Beehr and Gupta 1978; Farris 1971; Koch and Steers 1978; Siegel and Ruh 1973; Wickert 1951). However, the relationship between job involvement and turnover is moderated by other factors, the nature of which are not well understood. Farris (1971), for instance, found a negative relationship between the two variables among workers of a pharmaceutical company, but failed to find a similar relationship among engineers of an electronic firm. One could explain the discrepancy in terms of the professional involvement, as opposed to the job involvement, of engineers. As Baba (1979) pointed out,

"Engineers identify themselves more in terms of their profession than in terms of their employing organization. They are likely to continue their involvement in their profession even if they switch organizations" (p. 18). Such an interpretation, however, raises issues of construct validity for the concept of job involvement and its relation to both professional and organizational involvement of workers. These issues have to be resolved before one can understand how job involvement affects worker turnover.

Absenteeism

As a form of withdrawal behavior, absenteeism of workers should be influenced by job involvement. Highly involved workers should exhibit lower levels of absenteeism. Three empirical studies (Beehr and Gupta 1978; Patchen 1970; Saal 1978) reported a significant negative relationship between the two variables. Siegel and Ruh (1973), however, reported an insignificant relationship. On the basis of the existing evidence, it seems reasonable to assume a negative relationship between job involvement and absenteeism, but the evidence is limited to only a few studies. Clearly, more research needs to be done using different indexes of absenteeism before one can put confidence in the nature of the relationship. Absenteeism manifests itself in various forms. Workers may remain absent for health reasons or may remain absent just to avoid work. It is the latter form of absenteeism that should be negatively related to job involvement. Future studies should pay closer attention to the nature of absenteeism while relating it to job involvement.

The psychological approach to job involvement described in this chapter is characterized by conceptual ambiguities with respect to the nature of job involvement and contradictions and confusions with respect to empirical findings about the correlates (including the causes and effects of job involvement. In a sense, the psychological approach has put the cart before the horse by actively pursuing numerous empirical studies on the correlates of job involvement without first carefully examining the conceptual and operational phases of the constructs. Consequently, there is hardly any agreement among psychologists with regard to the nature of job involvement. For some psychologists (Lodahl and Kejner 1965; Saleh and Hosek 1976) job involvement is multidimensional in character, whereas for others (Lawler and Hall 1970) it is a unidimensional attitude. Some view job involvement as a stable personal characteristic (Lodahl and Kejner 1965; Runyon 1973), whereas others view it as situationally determined (Vroom 1969). Still others view job involvement as determined by an interaction of both person and situation (Lawler and Hall 1970).

In spite of such differences in the conceptualization of job involvement, there is one common thread that runs through all the psychological formulations outlined above. All seem to emphasize that situations lacking in opportunity for the satisfaction of intrinsic needs of the individual (such as self-esteem, achievement, autonomy, control, self-expression, and self-actualization) will decrease the individual's involvement. Even the recent studies on central life interest in work settings, on organizational identification, and on organizational commitment (Dubin, Champoux, and Porter 1975; Hall and Schneider 1972; Hall, Schneider, and Nygren 1970) reflect this bias. Lack of intrinsic-need satisfaction appears to be the basic condition for increasing work alienation. In this regard, psychologists seem to have followed the sociological tradition of considering the lack of individual freedom, power, and control as necessary preconditions of the psychological state of alienation. The exclusive emphasis on intrinsic motivation in explaining work alienation and a total lack of interest in extrinsic motivation among researchers stem from the humanistic conceptualization of human nature (Maslow 1954; McGregor 1960). Both theories of worker alienation and techniques to measure the phenomenon have been heavily biased in favor of humanistic thinking that emphasizes the role of intrinsic-growth needs (so called higher-order needs). To what extent this position is theoretically and methodologically sound and generalizable across cultures is an issue that will be examined in subsequent chapters.

5

THEORETICAL AND METHODOLOGICAL PROBLEMS

Mankind have long been convinced that $2 + 2 = 4$, . . .
but when people were asked what they meant . . . they
gave vague and divergent answers, which made it plain
that they did not know what these symbols meant.
Bertrand Russell, 1965

Reviews of both the sociological and the psychological literature on work alienation and involvement indicate the presence of a vast amount of theoretical and empirical literature on the subject (Blauner 1964; Durkheim 1893; Kanungo 1979, 1981; Marx 1932; Rabinowitz and Hall 1977; Seeman 1971; Shepard 1971). Yet, despite such rich literature, our understanding of the phenomenon of work alienation has not progressed beyond the superficial descriptive levels. The discussion of the literature in the preceding two chapters reveals that the concepts of work alienation and involvement and their correlates have been defined rather loosely by both sociologists and psychologists. Very often, social scientists have used the concepts of alienation and involvement to describe and explain work-related problems, such as low productivity, low morale, absenteeism, and turnover (Blauner 1964; Walton 1972) without seriously examining the precise nature of the concepts and their relationship to the characteristics of workers and work situations. This state of affairs has led both Seeman (1971) and Johnson (1973) to express their concern with the promiscuous usage of the concepts and the resulting difficulty in understanding their meaning. Because of loose usage in varied contexts, the concepts have come to carry excess meaning and very often different meanings for different researchers. Distorted and ambiguous interpretations of the concepts have created an aura of mysticism that must be dispelled before a scientific understanding of the phenomena can be achieved.

In the past two decades, literally hundreds of studies on work involvement and alienation have been reported. These studies were reviewed in the previous two chapters. Most of the studies have described the phenomena of alienation and involvement in varied work contexts and have explored the nature of their correlates. But only a few of these studies (Blauner 1964; Lawler and Hall 1970; Lodahl and Kejner 1965; Saleh and Hosek 1976; Shepard 1971) have attempted to define and operationalize the concepts. Even among these attempts at defining the concepts, there is no agreement on either the definition or the measurement of the concepts. Hardly any study has made an attempt to develop a unified theory of work alienation and involvement that would define the concepts more precisely within a single conceptual framework, determine ways of measuring the phenomena they represent, and relate them to their antecedent (causes) and consequent (effects) conditions.

The difficulty in developing a comprehensive theory of work involvement and alienation may have resulted from several conceptual and methodological problems constantly encountered by researchers in this area. In both the theoretical treatments of the concepts and their operationalization, one can notice the presence of several sources of confusion that have contributed to the exasperating conceptual ambiguity prevailing in the literature. Eight major sources of confusion that have caused problems for the researchers in the area are identified and discussed in the following section. It goes without saying that any meaningful scientific treatment of work alienation and involvement should in the future guard against these sources of confusion.

SOURCES OF CONFUSION

Equivocal Usage of the Concepts

The most common source of confusion can be found in the multiple usage of the concepts of work alienation and involvement. These concepts have been used by researchers to mean different things at different times. For instance, the concepts have sometimes been used to describe the psychological states of a specific individual worker and sometimes to describe the psychological states of groups of workers. Particularly in sociological writings one finds the use of the concept of alienation sometimes describing the psychological state of the individual and at other times describing pathological states of large collectivities, such as groups, organizations, and other sociopolitical systems. As Johnson (1973) correctly pointed out, "There is a difference in meaning between these two applications that is not merely the difference between singular and plural categories. The phenomenology and the meaning connected with individual states of alienation are different both in quality and significance from those connected with the social, interactional, and collective applications of the term" (p. 35). For example, to say that a worker is alienated can mean two things. It can suggest a collective experience of worker alienation, as reflected in absenteeism, tardiness, goldbricking, sabotage, and so on, that results from the prevailing social and physical conditions (mechanization, impersonal control through rules and regulations, and so on) within the organization; it can also suggest an individual worker's personal view of a job that does not meet salient needs (unique to the individual) regardless of how other workers view the situation. From a methodoligical standpoint, it is advisable to approach the study of alienation at the personal, rather than at the collective, level of experience. Measurement and interpretation of the collective experience of alienation are often difficult and confusing.

Measurement of the Concepts

A second source of confusion stems from the fact that the concept of alienation has been described and measured in two different ways. Sometimes the term alienation is used to imply objective social conditions directly observed by others and later attributed to individuals and groups. Among sociologists, Blauner (1964), for instance, considered mechanization and division of labor to be the alienating conditions, and people working under these conditions were assumed to be experiencing alienation. Likewise, several psychologists (Argyris 1964; McGregor 1960) have argued that the presence of certain organizational climates (nonparticipation, pyramidal values), certain management philosophies (Theory X assumptions), and certain job characteristics (repetition, routine, and so on) are good measures of alienating conditions. Workers experiencing these objective social conditions were assumed to be experiencing alienation at work.

In contrast to these attempts at viewing work alienation and involvement in terms of objective social and job conditions, there have been several attempts at interpreting and measuring the concepts as subjective psychological states of the individual worker. Such psychological states of the worker cannot be directly observed by outsiders, but are only experienced by the worker. Viewing work alienation in these two ways has obvious implications for the operationalization of the concept. States of alienation measured through the identification of objective conditions may not parallel the subjective measures of the concept. Mechanization, division of labor, or certain routine

aspects of a job in an organization may be viewed by external observers
as necessarily contributing to a state of alienation in the worker, such
as powerlessness or meaninglessness; but the worker may not perceive the situation in the same way. In fact, it is quite conceivable
that for some workers (mentally and physically handicapped, unskilled, uneducated, and many belonging to developing countries)
mechanization, division of labor, or a routine task may increase
rather than decrease job involvement. For instance, workers who
are mentally or physically handicapped, unskilled, or uneducated may
find routine and repetitive tasks less alienating than complex tasks
requiring varied skills. Likewise, mechanization and a division of
labor may create greater job involvement among many workers in developing countries who prefer clarity of job descriptions and bounded
responsibilities, presumably because of their authoritarian upbringing.

Failure to Distinguish the Phenomenon from Its Causes and Effects

A third source of confusion results from a failure on the part of
researchers to maintain the conceptual distinction between the state
of work alienation and its antecedent conditions on the one hand and
its consequent states on the other. Sometimes the confusion results
from mistaking the cause for the effect. Such mistakes are quite apparent in the case of those researchers who have used objective social
and job conditions as indexes of worker alienation. When worker
alienation is measured in terms of objectively observable physical
states of mechanization and divisions of labor (Blauner 1964) in an organization, the cause-and-effect distinction is blurred. Mechanization
and division of labor may be the environmental conditions or causes
of work alienation, but they do not represent a description of the state
of alienation itself.

Reflecting on the nature of the state of alienation, Josephson
and Josephson (1973) pointed out that

> such states, although functions of the conditions that pro-
> duce them, should not be confused with the conditions them-
> selves. For example, Durkheim's notion of anomie or
> normlessness can be regarded as an important cause of
> alienation but should not be confused with alienation as a
> state of mind. Similar considerations apply to other con-
> cepts which are often confused with alienation. To take
> another example, social isolation may lead to a state of
> estrangement, but not all isolates are alienated. Indeed,
> alienation may result from the social pressures of group,

crowd, or mass, as David Riesman and others have suggested. By the same token, alienation should not be confused with "social disorganization," since estrangement
may be found in highly organized bureaucracies. Alienation is often associated with loneliness, but, again, not
all lonely people are estranged. [P. 166]

In spite of such warnings, both the sociological and the psychological formulations neglect to maintain the distinction between alienating conditions and alienating states. In fact, most empirical researchers have attempted to measure the state of alienation through
indexes of alienating conditions instead of directly measuring it,
thinking that the two are equivalent. For instance, Seeman (1959)
considered normlessness to be the perception of a social situation in
which rules and norms regulating behavior had broken down. Such
perceptions may be the antecedent conditions of the alienated state,
but they cannot be identified with the alienated state itself. Likewise,
isolation, meaninglessness, and powerlessness may describe different conditions or causes of alienation, but should not be equated with
it. Even when self-estrangement was measured by Blauner (1964),
he used several indexes of alienating conditions of the job, such as
whether the job met the worker's achievement needs. Shepard (1971)
also measured the different forms of alienation suggested by Seeman
(1959) by measuring various job conditions, such as whether the job
provided opportunity for participation and control (powerlessness),
how the job fit into the total operation of the organization (meaninglessness), and the like. Clearly these kinds of questions probe into
the assumed conditions or causes of alienation, rather than into the
state of alienation itself.

In the psychological literature similar confusion is also noticed.
For instance, Saleh and Hosek (1976) have proposed a measure of job
involvement that contains three distinct categories of items. The
first category measures directly the state of alienation (with the item
"The most important things I do are involved with my job"). The
second category seems to index the antecedent conditions or presumed
causes of alienation (with the item "How much chance do you get to do
things your own way?"). Finally, a third category measures workers'
behaviors and experiences that often (but not necessarily) result from
the alienated state (with the item "I avoid taking on extra duties and
responsibilities in my work"). Thus, Saleh and Hosek combine indexes of causal conditions and effects of alienating states into one
single instrument. Such an instrument cannot provide meaningful
data on the state of alienation of the worker. Needless to say, for
both conceptual clarity and effective methodology in empirical studies,
the state of alienation needs to be identified and measured separately
from its causes, as well as its effects.

Nature of the Psychological State of Work Alienation

A fourth source of confusion results from the description of the
psychological state of work alienation as being both a cognitive and an
affective state of the worker. Most researchers have found it difficult
to strip the concept of work alienation from its negative affect. Traditionally, work alienation has been associated with negative emotional states, such as boredom, frustration, anger, and dissatisfaction experienced on the job. On the other hand, work involvement
has been associated with positive emotional states, such as excite-
ment, pleasantness, and satisfaction experienced on the job. Many
measures of work alienation or involvement, therefore, contain items
reflecting levels of job satisfaction or dissatisfaction (for example, the
item "The major satisfaction in my life comes from my job" in Lodahl
and Kejner 1965). Recent empirical studies (Lawler and Hall 1970;
Seeman 1971) clearly suggest that work involvement and job satisfaction
are not the same thing, although they may be related to one another.
It may be more useful to conceptualize the states of work involvement
or alienation as cognitive or belief states of identity or dissociation
(separateness) with work, rather than as psychological states necessarily associated with feelings of satisfaction or dissatisfaction on the
job. A cognitive state of dissociation may or may not accompany a
positive or negative affect under certain conditions. A highly involved
worker under some conditions may feel a high level of satisfaction
with work and under other conditions may experience deep dissatisfaction. In the future, empirical work needs to be done to identify
conditions under which work involvement and alienation are related
to positive, negative, and neutral affective states of workers. It
would also be of interest to explore the relationship of work alienation to the intensity of affective states experienced by workers.

Nature of Causation

The fifth source of confusion can be traced to the manner in
which the causes of work alienation have been conceptualized. Some
researchers have emphasized the characteristics of the work situation (situational variables discussed in the previous chapter) as the
major determinants of work alienation. Others have emphasized the
Protestant-work-ethic background as the major determinant of work
alienation. These two sets of determinants can be viewed as two kinds
of causation: contemporaneous and historical. They can also be described as precipitating and predisposing causes of work alienation.
The predisposing or historical causes of work alienation have to be
found in the past socialization history of the worker. For instance,

Lodahl and Kejner (1965) suggested that work involvement of an individual is determined by the early socialization process, during which the individual internalizes the values of the goodness of work or the Protestant ethic. In this sense, alienation from or involvement with work becomes a more stable characteristic of the individual, which carries from one situation to another.

Sociologists have viewed the historical causation of alienation in a slightly different way. Following Marx, many sociologists have considered job experience to be central to an individual's life. According to them, the longstanding social arrangements of technology, division of labor, and capitalist property institutions have created a state of alienation from work (Blauner 1964). Since work is central to one's life, alienation from work necessarily leads to alienation from all other aspects of life. As Seeman (1971) puts it, "Perhaps the most important thesis concerns the centrality of work experience, the imputation being that alienation from work 'is the core of all alienation' and that the consequences of alienated labor color the life space of the individual in a profound and disturbing way" (p. 135).

The state of alienation has also been conceived of as being caused by contemporaneous events or precipitating factors. For instance, Lawler and Hall (1970) consider the job-involved person to be one who is "affected very much by his whole job situation, presumably because he perceives his job as an important part of his self-concept and perhaps as a place to satisfy his important needs (e.g., his need for self-esteem)" (pp. 310-11). These authors, therefore, consider the worker's present perceptions of the need-satisfying potentialities of the job to be a major determinant of the state of involvement. From the above discussion, it is apparent that a state of work alienation or involvement may be jointly caused by two sets of events—one a historical or predisposing set of events and the other a contemporaneous or precipitating set of events. Through the socialization process (cumulative learning and experience of the past) the individual may develop a set of relatively stable beliefs and values regarding work, and the present experiences with work may either reinforce the beliefs and values or modify them.

Distinguishing Work Alienation and
Involvement from Intrinsic Motivation

An important source of ambiguity regarding the nature of work alienation stems from the fact that work involvement has typically been related to the satisfaction of intrinsic rather than extrinsic needs. As documented in the previous two chapters, both sociologists and psychologists have made repeated assertions that greater alienation or lower involvement results only when job situations lack the opportunity for satisfaction of intrinsic needs, such as self-esteem, achievement, autonomy, control, and self-actualization. In fact, intrinsic motivation and involvement have often been used synonymously, because both psychologists and sociologists have assumed that a person's involvement in a job will be a function of intrinsic factors, such as interesting work and the independence and responsibility of the job, rather than extrinsic factors, such as pay, security, and comfortable working conditions. This has led to the suggestion that where job design provided greater responsibility and autonomy on the job, workers were likely to be more involved in their jobs (Herzberg 1968; Lawler and Hall 1970).

This position, however, can be criticized (Gorn and Kanungo 1980; Kanungo 1979, 1981) on the grounds that satisfaction of intrinsic needs on the job may be a sufficient but not a necessary condition for work involvement. While satisfaction of intrinsic needs, such as the need for self-esteem or self-actualization, might increase the likelihood of work involvement, it neither characterizes nor defines the state of work involvement itself. Thus, a conceptual distinction should be made between intrinsic motivation and job involvement, a distinction supported by the work of Lawler and Hall (1970). Such a distinction is particularly warranted given the possibility that the direct link between intrinsic motivation and the creation of high involvement may not be as strong as previously believed. It is quite likely that involvement in work may depend upon the degree to which the job is perceived to meet salient needs, be they intrinsic or extrinsic.

Distinguishing Different Aspects of
Work Involvement and Alienation

Up to this point in the book, the terms work and job have been used synonymously. This was done on purpose to reflect the common usage of the terms. Both in sociological and psychological literature, one finds such synonymous usage of the two terms very common. However, the use of the terms in a synonymous fashion has caused considerable confusion in our understanding and measurement of work-alienation phenomena. The concept of "work" is complex, more general, and includes many specific identifiable components. For instance, involvement with or alienation from work may include involvement with or alienation from work in general (Blood 1969; Wollack, Goodale, Wijting, and Smith 1971), occupation (Faunce 1959), organization (Dubin, Champoux, and Porter 1975), or job (Lodahl and Kejner 1965).

Most researchers, while dealing with the problem of worker alienation, have failed to differentiate the various components of work toward which a worker may show alienation or involvement. Take, for instance, two of the components: involvement or alienation in a particular job and relative involvement or alienation with work in general in comparison with other activities (for example, family, leisure). These are two different attitudes, and presumably they are determined by different sets of antecedent conditions. While previous researchers have discussed both of these aspects of the phenomenon, they have not treated them as distinct notions (Lodahl and Kejner 1965; Rabinowitz and Hall 1977). For instance, in developing a measure for job involvement, Lodahl and Kejner (1965) included items that reflected both aspects. Items such as "I'll stay overtime to finish a job even if I am not paid for it" would tend to measure involvement in a particular job. On the other hand, items such as "To me work is only a small part of who I am" would reflect an individual's involvement with work in general relative to other nonwork activities.

In research literature, the phenomenon of alienation or involvement is sometimes conceptualized as the perceived importance of work in one's life or the degree of psychological identification with work (Kanungo 1979; Rabinowitz and Hall 1977). With this conceptualization, emphasis is placed more on involvement with work in general than on involvement in a particular job. Involvement in this sense is considered a product of the Protestant-ethic type of socialization and, hence, a characteristic that an individual presumably carries from one job situation to another. At other times, the phenomenon of alienation or involvement is characterized as the importance of or psychological identification with one's present job. Involvement in a particular job, therefore, may be somewhat different from the individual's involvement with work in general. Involvement in a particular job is determined by a person's job situation. Active involvement in a job should be dependent upon whether that particular job satisfies one's salient needs. The validity of such a distinction between particular job involvement and general work involvement has been tested recently by Gorn and Kanungo (1980) and will be discussed in detail in a later chapter.

Lack of an Integrative Approach

The final source of confusion in our understanding of the alienation phenomena stems from the parting of the ways between sociological and psychological research. The two lines of research run parallel to each other, and little attempt has been made to bring them together. As a result, work-alienation literature harbors a large number of both psychological and sociological explanatory and descriptive constructs without any attempt at parsimony and integration.

A close examination of the sociological and psychological approaches shows that they differ on three fronts. First, there is an emphasis in sociological writings (Marx 1932; Seeman 1971) on the analysis and measurement of the state of alienation among workers, whereas in psychological writings (Lawler and Hall 1970; Saleh and Hosek 1976) the emphasis is on the analysis and measurement of the state of involvement. Sociologists with a clinical perspective have been concerned with identifying conditions and consequences of the state of work alienation, whereas psychologists have been concerned with identifying conditions and consequences of the state of work involvement. In a sense sociologists have dealt with the negative side of the issue, and psychologists have dealt with the positive side. The two approaches seem to complement one another, and yet, at first glance they appear quite divergent. As a result the interface between the two approaches has never been examined.

A second difference between the two approaches stems from the fact that the sociological treatment of work alienation considers the phenomena at the group or social-system level, whereas the psychological treatment of work involvement concentrates on analysis at the individual level. For this reason, sociologists in their analysis often use terms that represent collective phenomena, such as labor alienation or urban alienation. Psychologists, on the other hand, analyze the phenomena in terms of psychological states of individual workers.

Finally, in describing the phenomena, sociologists are more inclined to use "epiphenomenal categories," such as "loneliness," "normlessness," or "isolation" (Johnson 1973b), whereas psychologists restrict the description to behavioral terms, such as working overtime, participating in the decision-making process, or feeling satisfied at work (Saleh and Hosek 1976). Epiphenomenal abstractions in sociological writings represent attempts at collectively summarizing and classifying a series of specific behaviors under single categories. Such abstractions stand in clear contrast to psychological descriptions of the phenomena purely in terms of specific behavior. Differences in the levels of analysis and in the usage of descriptive terminology representing different levels of abstraction have created difficulties in achieving an integration of the psychological and sociological approaches. Because of the lack of integration, psychologists and sociologists have failed to understand one another and, consequently, have ignored valuable literature outside their own discipline.

PROBLEMS WITH MEASUREMENT
OF JOB INVOLVEMENT

The confusions surrounding the concepts of job and work alienation discussed above have spread to the measurement of the phenomena. This has caused two types of problems: the problem of construct validity of the measuring instruments and the problem of interpretation of results of empirical studies that used these instruments.

The Problem of Construct Validity

The constructs of job and work alienation have been formulated in such a way that they tend to carry excess meaning (for example, job involvement means both the psychological identification with a job and the performance-self-esteem contingency). Consequently, the techniques developed to measure the constructs suffer from the problems of construct validity. For instance, the most widely used job-involvement scale (Lodahl and Kejner 1965) contains items designed to measure both psychological identification and performance-self-esteem contingency notions. But these are two distinct notions, and Lodahl and Kejner do not provide any explanation regarding how to interpret the relationship between the two notions. As Siegel (1971) pointed out, Lodahl and Kejner "never address themselves to the issue of whether or not they expect the various items of the involvement scale to be correlated or whether they feel that they are tapping distinct job attitudes as their two definitions imply. This seems to leave a major point unanswered since the goal of this research is to gain as clear a conceptualization as possible concerning what attitudes and feeling states the construct involvement is actually measuring" (p. 21). The same problem was noticed by Rabinowitz and Hall (1977), who stated that "although Lodahl and Kejner's factor analyses revealed the multidimensional nature of job involvement, these different dimensions have never been clearly identified and labeled. Most later researchers have taken a few items from Lodahl and Kejner's questionnaire, with no consideration of what factor they loaded on, and then called their scale 'job involvement.' To date, there is still no agreement on just what the Lodahl and Kejner job involvement scale really is!" (p. 270). (For the sake of the reader's review, the items contained in Lodahl and Kejner's scale (1965) are presented in Appendix A.)

More recently, Saleh and Hosek (1976) have developed a new job-involvement scale containing 30 items. On the basis of factor analysis, these 30 items were selected from a total pool of 65 items taken from the work of earlier researchers (Davis 1966; Dubin 1956; French and Kahn 1962; Iverson and Reuder 1956; Lodahl and Kejner 1965; Vroom 1962, 1964; Wickert 1951). Saleh and Hosek (1976) maintained that their 30-item scale measured three dimensions of job involvement, such as active participation in the job, perception of work as a central life interest, and perception of job performance as central to self-esteem. As was pointed out earlier, the notion of job involvement as a psychological identification or central life interest should not be confused with the notion of intrinsic motivation on the job. But the Saleh and Hosek scale puts the two notions together as dimensions of job involvement and confuses the two issues. For instance, the item "How much chance do you get to do things your own way?" is a measure of perceived autonomy on the job. Saleh and Hosek consider it as an "active participation item." It is also an item designed to measure intrinsic-need satisfaction on the job. Saleh and Hosek have included the item in their job-involvement scale because they assumed that a worker who finds greater autonomy on the job is necessarily more job involved. But this is not necessarily true, because greater autonomy would lead to greater involvement only for intrinsically motivated workers whose autonomy needs are very strong and salient and not for extrinsically motivated workers. (The items in the Saleh and Hosek scale are presented in Appendix A for the reader's review.)

Both the most widely used Lodahl and Kejner scale (1965) and the most recent Saleh and Hosek scale (1976) exclude the possibility of finding extrinsically motivated workers to be more job involved. Both the scales are insensitive to the logical distinction between intrinsic motivation and involvement made earlier in this chapter. A similar problem is noticed in the scales developed by sociologists to measure alienation. For instance, Shepard (1971) constructed separate scales to measure different forms of alienation suggested by Seeman (1959) using both blue-collar and white-collar samples. His scales include many items that measure intrinsic motivation. His "powerlessness scale" includes items that measure the level of autonomy and control, and his "meaninglessness scale" contains items that measure the level of feedback workers get from their work environment. (The items from Shepard's scales are presented in Appendix A.)

It may be pointed out that all three scales suffer from another common problem. Each scale has used the terms job and work rather loosely. In each scale, some items make reference to involvement with work in general, and other items make reference to involvement in specific job situations. Among the five scales developed by Shepard (1971), two (the instrumental work orientation and self-evaluative involvement scales) have items that make explicit reference to "occupations" (as a surrogate for work in general), rather than to specific jobs. On the grounds of both the failure to distinguish involvement from intrinsic motivation and the failure to consistently use a single context (job or work or occupation) while measuring workers' involvement, the construct validity of the existing scales is questionable.

Problems of Interpretation of Empirical Data

Problems of construct validity of measures of job involvement necessarily lead to problems of interpretation of results in studies that use these measures. It seems that the results of many psychological and sociological studies of job involvement and their correlates (including causes and effects) reviewed in the preceding chapter reflect more artifacts than true relationships. For instance, Table 5.1 presents a summary of the approximate magnitude of relationship of job involvement with some of its correlates taken from a recent textbook in organizational behavior (Chung and Megginson 1981, p. 396). Table 5.1 shows that job involvement is positively related to several task attributes, such as autonomy, task variety, and feedback, and to individual factors, such as achievement needs, Protestant ethic, and job skills. On the basis of such results, other textbooks (Steers 1981) confidently conclude that "many employees today are unable to identify with the work they do or with their employer. They work on jobs that have little meaning and under conditions over which they have little control. As such, it is not surprising to find workers who are alienated and dissatisfied" (p. 10).

Such generalized conclusions and the results on which they are based are questionable on the basis of two major problems inherent in the studies of job involvement. The first problem stems from the use of measures that do not differentiate job involvement from intrinsic motivation. The magnitude of relationship reported in Table 5.1 is derived from studies using the Lodahl and Kejner (1965) or Saleh

TABLE 5.1

Correlates of Job Involvement and the Approximate
Magnitude of Relationship

Job characteristics	
Task variety	.24
Task identity	.20
Autonomy	.27
Feedback	.30
Goal setting	.50
Personal characteristics	
Achievement needs	.40
Protestant ethic	.40
Job skills	+

and Hosek (1976) job-involvement scales. Since these scales themselves include several items that measure intrinsic motivation (participation, autonomy, use of abilities at work, and so on), it is quite possible that studies using these scales will consistently find a positive relationship between job involvement and certain job and personal correlates that represent intrinsic-type rewards (task, variety, autonomy, and so on) or needs (achievement need, Protestant ethic, and so on).

Thus, the magnitude of relationship reported in Table 5.1 is more a function of intrinsic-motivation items included in job-involvement scales than a function of the construct of job involvement. If one distinguishes job involvement from intrinsic motivation by defining it as a pure psychological state of identification with the job and measures the construct as such, then one may find different magnitudes of relationship than those presented in Table 5.1.

This issue was addressed in a recent study by Saal (1981), who measured job involvement in two different ways and explored the relationship of the two measures to some of the task and personal attributes listed in Table 5.1. The two measures of job involvement used by Saal were the 20-item Lodahl and Kejner scale (1965), which contains intrinsic motivation items, and a 3-item scale (items chosen from Lodahl and Kejner 1965), which measures job involvement as purely a psychological state of identification with job. Saal's results indicate that the magnitude of relationship is substantially lower in the case of the 3-item scale than in the case of the 20-item scale. For instance, in a stepwise regression analysis, Saal found that while the feedback variable explained 15 percent of the variance in job involvement when measured by Lodahl and Kejner's 20-item scale, it explained only 7 percent of the variance in job involvement measured by the 3-item scale. In fact, the values of R^2 associated with the regression equations derived to predict psychological identification with the job measured by the three-item scale were consistently smaller. In other words, job involvement as a psychological state of identification appeared much less predictable from a knowledge of intrinsic task and personal characteristics than the data in Table 5.1 might suggest.

The second major problem with the interpretation of empirical results in the field stems from the culture-based characteristics of the U.S. samples used in most studies. The reportedly low, but positive, relationship between job involvement as a psychological state of identification and job or personal attributes representing intrinsic rewards or needs may partly result from the dominant work values of U.S. workers. Most studies that have argued in favor of stable, positive relationships (Saal 1981) have used samples of U.S. workers who live in a society that values intrinsic needs and rewards more than extrinsic needs and rewards. These workers are more likely to consider intrinsic needs as more salient in their lives than extrinsic needs, and, therefore, it is possible that these workers would show greater psychological identification with their jobs when their jobs offered them more intrinsic outcomes, such as autonomy and achievement. Such relationships, however, may not hold true for workers belonging to other cultures holding opposite sets of values with regard to job outcomes. In order to find out the true relationship of job involvement with its task and personal correlates, one needs to assess and, if possible, eliminate the confounding effects of the culture bias of respondents. This can be done only through the use of cross-cultural samples in studies on job involvement.

6

A REFORMULATION:
THE MOTIVATIONAL
APPROACH

Simple statements, if knowledge is our object, are to be
prized more highly than less simple ones because they
tell us more; because their empirical content is greater;
and because they are better testable.

K. Popper, 1959

INTRODUCTION

Empirical research on worker alienation and involvement in
both sociological and psychological literature is fraught with conceptual ambiguities. In addition, instruments developed to measure work
alienation and involvement often contain inherent methodological in-
adequacies, since they are based on constructs that are conceptually
ambiguous. Results of studies dealing with these phenomena, therefore, are difficult to interpret. The identification of some major conceptual and methodological problems and the discussion of the difficulty in interpretation of empirical results in the previous chapter
make it clear that in the future any meaningful and systematic progress in our understanding of the phenomena must come from a theoretical reformulation of the issue. Such a formulation, called the
motivational approach, is presented in this chapter.

It would not be an overstatement to suggest that in the area of
work alienation there is an urgent need for a revised conceptual framework that should have the ability to integrate, in a parsimonious way,
diverse thinking on the subject. In addition to the qualities of integration and parsimony, the framework should also have a greater
cross-cultural generality. The motivational approach described in
this chapter offers such a framework. As a conceptual framework,
the major objectives of the motivational approach are to integrate the

two parallel streams of psychological and sociological thought on work alienation and involvement; to describe, explain, measure, and predict the phenomena in the most simple and parsimonious way using existing psychological theories of human motivation, attitudes, and behavior; and to provide a cross-cultural perspective to the study and measurement of work-alienation phenomena without any cultural bias. By providing an integrative model, the motivational approach aims at helping researchers in the fields of psychology and sociology to speak a common language while dealing with problems of work alienation and involvement and to benefit from each other's work in the area. By providing a parsimonious model, the approach aims at getting rid of the excess meaning attached to the concepts themselves (alienation and involvement) and to their explanations (psychological and socio-logical). By providing a model with a broader cross-cultural general-ity, the approach aims at removing the culturally contaminated and myopic view of alienation (that intrinsic motivation and the Protestant ethic are necessary conditions for involvement) and at encouraging the development of measurement techniques free of cultural bias.

THE MOTIVATIONAL APPROACH

The conceptual framework suggested here for future studies of work alienation and involvement is called the motivational approach for the simple reason that it uses the existing motivational language in psychology to explain the phenomena. There are two main reasons for using the existing motivational language over other forms of so-ciological (powerlessness, meaninglessness, and so on) and psycho-logical (person- or situation-specific correlates) descriptions. First, theories of human motivation at work (Maslow 1954; Lawler 1973) are generally advanced to explain all work behavior, and alienation and involvement at work should not be considered exceptions. Second, the fact that the existing motivational constructs can adequately and parsimoniously explain work-alienation phenomena lies hidden in many of the sociological and psychological formulations discussed earlier. Thus, a clearer motivational formulation of the phenomena is needed to bring this fact to the surface. In addition to the use of motivational language, the motivational approach is characterized by an emphasis on seven other considerations described in the following paragraphs.

In the motivational approach, the concepts of involvement and alienation are viewed as opposite sides of the same phenomenon. Sociologists have consistently used the term alienation, and psycho-logists have consistently used the term involvement while studying work behavior. On the surface they seem to have ignored each other's work, thinking that they are dealing with two distinct types of behavioral phenomena. On closer examination, however, it is quite evident that both psychologists and sociologists are dealing with the same psychological states of individual workers. Psychologists clearly consider work involvement as a psychological state of the worker. Sociologists, on the other hand, describe the phenomenon of alienation at the collective level (alienation of labor) and sometimes interpret the phenomenon as a psychological state of individual workers and at other times as objective social conditions (such as social disorganization or anomie). The empirically oriented sociologists have found it difficult to measure and interpret objective social conditions as an index of work alienation. Recently, therefore, many sociologists (Seeman 1959, 1971; Shepard 1971) have come to recognize the fact that the phenomenon of work alienation can best be described and measured as the psychological states of workers. If both alienation and involvement refer to psychological states of the individual, it would be more parsimonious and appropriate to consider the concepts as representing opposite ends of a single psychological dimension rather than to consider them as independent dimensions. Thus, alienation and involvement may be considered as unidimensional and bipolar constructs.

Since the motivational approach views work alienation in terms of psychological states of individual workers, it limits itself to the analysis of the behavioral phenomenon at the individual level. Many sociologists have described work alienation at a collective level. They have followed Marx, who popularized the notion that capitalism produces mass labor alienation. Closer scrutiny of the recent empirical work of sociologists (Blauner 1964; Clark 1959; Shepard 1971) shows, however, that they limit themselves to the analysis of the work-related behavior of individual workers. The Marxian notion of labor alienation cannot be studied at an empirical level without the observation and analysis of the individual worker's behavior. Therefore, for empirical analysis and operationalization of the constructs, an individual level of analysis is preferable to a collective level of analysis.

The motivational approach identifies the states of alienation and involvement with the cognitive belief states of the workers. As a cognitive state, alienation or involvement of workers becomes conceptually distinct from many associated covert feelings or affective states expressed in terms of satisfactions or dissatisfactions experienced by the workers in work or job contexts. Thus, job satisfaction as an affective state is clearly distinguished from alienation or involvement, which represents a belief state. Many social scientists (Seeman 1959; Weissenberg and Gruenfeld 1968) equate job involvement with intrinsic-need satisfaction on the job. They consider job satisfaction to be distinct from job involvement only when job satisfaction represents extrinsic-need satisfaction. The present formulation, however, considers job satisfaction to include the affective states of both intrinsic- and extrinsic-need satisfaction. It distinguishes job involvement from job satisfaction only on the basis that the former is a cognitive belief state and the latter is an affective state of the workers. In this sense, the motivational approach adheres to the Hegelian notion of alienation as a purely cognitive state of separation and, thus, avoids the confusion created by the Marxian notion, which equates intrinsic-job satisfaction with job involvement.

By considering involvement-alienation as a cognitive belief state, the motivational approach not only distinguishes it from other associated affective states but also distinguishes it from other associated overt behavior, such as worker participation, assumption of additional responsibilities, or acceptance of working overtime without financial rewards. While such overt behaviors may represent states of involvement for some workers (those belonging to cultures that place a high value on work behavior directed at satisfying intrinsic needs), they may not represent states of involvement for other workers (those belonging to cultures that do not value such behavior).

The motivational approach emphasizes that involvement-alienation as a cognitive belief state of workers must be clearly distinguished from its causes (antecedent conditions) and its effects (consequent conditions). It considers the phenomenon to be caused by both historical and contemporary events. In order to determine the historical causes of alienation, one has to look for causal factors in the early socialization process of workers. To discover the contemporary causes of the phenomenon, one needs to look into the immediate social and work-related contexts. Besides identifying the two types of causes of the cognitive belief state of alienation, the motivational approach also stresses that the state of alienation has significant effects on subsequent job and work behavior and attitudes. In fact, according to the motivational approach, no specific behavioral act or attitude can be assumed to necessarily follow from the state of alienation. Therefore, it is important that future research in the area of work alienation establishes contingencies of relationship between the state of alienation and a specific behavior or attitude of workers. For instance, future research may find that the state of job involvement of workers results in increased participation or overtime work without pay only under certain conditions. Under other conditions such behavioral effects may not be noticed among job-involved workers.

Unlike most sociologists and psychologists who often view involvement-alienation in work contexts as equivalent to intrinsic motivation of workers, the motivational approach argues for maintaining a conceptual distinction between the two. In the sociological literature, such a distinction was hinted at by Becker and Carper (1956). These authors distinguished two sources of occupational identification: through job title and through growth and development at work. Workers' identification through job title represents their cognitive state of job involvement, whereas their sense of job commitment resulting from growth and development at work represents their intrinsic motivation. In psychological literature, Lawler and Hall (1970) advocated a distinction between job involvement and intrinsic motivation. According to Lawler and Hall, "Job involvement may be thought of as the degree to which the job situation is central to the person and his identity. Intrinsic motivation can be thought of as the degree to which attaining higher order need satisfaction depends upon performance" (p. 311). The usefulness of such a distinction for job and work-flow design has been demonstrated recently by Moch (1980). On the basis of his study covering 522 employees of an assembly and packaging plant, Moch concluded that "it seems clear that job involvement is distinctly different from internal motivation. Variables which seem to lead to internal motivation do not appear to facilitate job involvement; some of them actually inhibit it" (p. 28). Along the same line, the motivational approach argues that the cognitive state of involvement or alienation is not exclusively dependent on intrinsic-need satisfaction at work. Sometimes satisfaction of intrinsic needs of the workers through job performance might increase the likelihood of their job involvement, but it does not define job involvement itself. Such a distinction between the two constructs—involvement and intrinsic motivation—is essential in view of the fact that one may cause the other.

Implicit in the study of the phenomenon of involvement-alienation is the question, Who or what are the subject and the object of alienation? The subject is the person who is alienated, and the object is something from which the person is alienated. The motivational approach emphasizes the necessity for clearly specifying both the subject and the object of alienation. In the context of work alienation, most researchers agree on who the subject is. The subject is the individual worker (or the worker's self). But the specification of the object of alienation has been a major source of confusion among researchers. Most previous studies in the area have used job, work, and occupation almost interchangeably as the object of alienation. Closer scrutiny makes it obvious that these concepts are not synonymous. In the motivational approach, distinctions are made between cognitive states of involvement-alienation from the job, the organization, the occupation (or profession), and work (or work role in general relative to other roles, such as in family, community, or leisure contexts). Each of the above concepts can serve as distinct objects of involvement-alienation and, therefore, should not be confused with one another.

In the empirical research literature, the concepts of "job" and "work" have been used widely and interchangeably. The motivational approach specifically deals with these two concepts as two separate components, each with distinct characteristics of its own. For instance, job as an object of alienation refers to the present job that a worker holds in a specific organization as described by the worker's job title (for example, assistant to the president of a given organization). On the other hand, work as an object of alienation refers to a much broader and more abstract concept. Alienation from work implies that the work role in general is considered of little importance to an individual when compared with other roles in his or her life, such as in family, community, and leisure contexts. In a sense, alienation from the present job refers to a cognitive belief that is descriptive of workers' relations with their present jobs. Hence, job alienation to a large extent is determined by existing perceived job characteristics. Alienation from work, on the other hand, refers to a normative belief. It is a cognitive belief of the individual regarding how much importance one should attach to work roles in one's life. Such a value-oriented normative belief is generally determined by one's past and present socialization experiences and reference-group influences.

Finally, the motivational approach has the potential to integrate and explain adequately the different types of alienation proposed by sociologists. Using simple motivational constructs, the motivational approach provides a parsimonious model that integrates both sociological and psychological interpretations of work alienation.

As the preceding discussion indicates, the framework provided by the motivational approach tries to overcome most of the problems identified in the previous chapter and, at the same time, to provide a parsimonious and unified theoretical formulation by integrating the psychological and sociological approaches.

Definitions of the Concepts

Within the framework of the motivational approach, the concepts of involvement and alienation are viewed as opposite sides of the same phenomenon. The phenomenon refers to psychological states of an individual worker and is conceived as cognitive and unidimensional in nature.

In the motivational approach, a distinction is made between involvement with or alienation from work in general and involvement with or alienation from a specific job. Involvement with work in general is viewed as a generalized cognitive (or belief) state of psychological identification with work, insofar as work is perceived to have the potential to satisfy one's salient needs and expectations. Likewise, work alienation can be viewed as a generalized cognitive (or belief) state of psychological separation from work, insofar as work is perceived to lack the potential for satisfying one's salient needs and expectations. Worker involvement with or alienation from a given job is defined as a specific cognitive belief state of psychological identification with or separation from that job. Here again, the state of involvement or alienation depends on two things: the saliency of the worker's needs (both extrinsic and intrinsic) and the expectations the worker has about the need-satisfying potential of the job. Thus, for both objects of alienation, specific job and work in general, the degree of involvement-alienation should be measured by the workers' cognitions about their identification with or separation from the objects.

Job- and work-involvement beliefs differ in two ways. First, job involvement refers to a specific belief regarding the present job, whereas work involvement refers to a general belief. The two beliefs also operate at different levels. The job-involvement belief operates at a descriptive level. It describes workers' job identifications as they they are. The work-involvement belief, on the other hand, operates at a normative level. It describes workers' views of their relationship with work as it should be. Since the objects of the two beliefs belong to the same universe (in which a job represents a specific category of work in general), some degree of positive relationship between the two beliefs is expected. A person who shows a high degree of work involvement is expected to show a high degree of job involvement. However, since the two beliefs operate at two different levels, the relationship between the two beliefs may not be strong. A person who thinks work should be considered very important in one's life may not necessarily find a specific job very involving.

The distinction between job and work involvement has several implications for future research. First, there is a need to develop separate measures of job and work involvement, the former representing a specific belief about a particular job, and the latter representing a general belief about work roles in general (as opposed to other roles in life, such as in family, community, and other leisure contexts). Second, it is important to discover how the two types of beliefs are related. It is quite conceivable that a person who is highly involved in work because of a Protestant-ethic upbringing may not feel involved with a particular job, since the job does not meet salient needs. Likewise, a person who is highly involved with a job because of salient-need satisfaction on the job may not consider work roles as being as central to life as other social roles. Because the two types of beliefs are conceptually different, it is necessary to identify conditions under which they do or do not covary. One such condition has recently been identified (Gorn and Kanungo 1980) and will be discussed in detail later. It has been suggested that for extrinsically motivated workers job and work involvement would tend to covary (with job satisfaction acting as a moderator variable), whereas for intrinsically motivated workers job and work involvement tend not to covary. Third, there is also a need for determining how job and work involvement influence involvement in other aspects of one's life, such as family involvement or community involvement. The Marxian dictum that work alienation is the root of all other forms of alienation in life has yet to be tested. It is quite conceivable that too much involvement in a particular job may alienate one from other activities, such as those in the family or community. On the other hand, an attitude of involvement with work roles in general may transfer positive effects to other aspects of life, as Marx predicted.

The motivational framework treats the concepts of involvement and alienation as cognitive states of an individual. Viewed in this manner, job and work involvement or job and work alienation cannot be measured with existing instruments (Blauner 1964; Lodahl and Kejner 1965; Saleh and Hosek 1976; Shepard 1971). Most of these instruments combine measures of the cognitive state of alienation with measures of its presumed causes and effects. For example, the widely used instrument developed by Lodahl and Kejner (1965) contains items that reflect the cognitive state of involvement ("I live, eat, and breathe my job") and also items that reflect both antecedent and consequent feeling states and behavioral tendencies ("I feel depressed when I fail at something connected with my job" or "I will stay overtime to finish a job, even if I am not paid for it"). Because of such built-in ambiguities in existing instruments, the data provided by these instruments are often hard to interpret. Future research should develop less ambiguous measures of job and work involvement (that is, measures reflecting only the cognitive state of psychological identification with job and work). For instance, items such as "I live, eat, and breathe my job," "I am very much involved in my job," "The most important thing that happened to me involved my job," and so on tend to reflect workers' awareness of job identification without measuring their need states (antecedent conditions), covert feelings, and overt behavioral tendencies (consequent conditions). These kinds of items have construct validity and, therefore, are more desirable measures of the cognitive state of job involvement. Similar items reflecting the cognitive state of identification with work in general can be used to measure work involvement.

One can also use graphic techniques or the semantic-differential format (Osgood, Suci, and Tannenbaum 1957) to measure job or work involvement on dimensions such as involved-noninvolved, important-unimportant, identified-separated, and central-peripheral. Besides being less confusing with regard to assessing the cognitive states of involvement and alienation, measures of job or work involvement that have construct validity seem to be better suited for cross-cultural and comparative research than are the existing measures. The existing measures are inappropriate for cross-cultural research primarily because they include many items that heavily emphasize intrinsic-need satisfaction. For groups of people who do not consider intrinsic needs (autonomy, control, and so on) to be the guiding forces in their lives, the existing measures cannot truly reflect their job or work involvement.

In defining involvement or alienation as cognitive beliefs of workers, the motivational approach emphasizes the fact that such beliefs are central to and have a major impact on workers' lives. The potential importance of beliefs regarding job and work involvement is quite obvious from the fact that people devote considerable time and effort to jobs and what they consider work roles (as opposed to other social roles). In a sense, as Saleh (1981) suggests, such beliefs are "self-involving," implying that they are not peripheral but central or core beliefs representing an individual's self. They define one's self-concept in a major way. Popularly we talk of an "organization man," "family man," "religious man," and so on depending on the individual's identification with an organization, family, religion, and so on. Likewise, we talk of "hard-working persons" (persons who believe in the value of hard work in their lives) or "persons married to their jobs." Such descriptions reflect our definitions of a personal self. As an individual, one defines personal self as an entity or develops a personal self-concept (an answer to the question, Who am I?) through identification with or alienation from major environmental objects, such as job, work, family, and religion. Such a self-concept (or underlying belief) has a regulating influence on individuals' behaviors and attitudes.

Conditions of Job Involvement

A layout of the present motivational approach to job involvement, its causes, and its effects is presented in Figure 6.1. As can be seen, individuals' behaviors and attitudes exhibited both on and off the job are a function of the saliency of need states within them. At any given moment, the need saliency within individuals depends on the prior socialization process (historical causation) and on the perceived potential of the environment (job, family, and so on) to satisfy the needs (contemporary causation). The cognitive state of involvement as a by-product of need saliency also depends on the nature of need saliency as historically determined through the socialization process and on the perceived potential of the environment to satisfy the needs.

FIGURE 6.1

The Motivational Approach to Involvement and Alienation

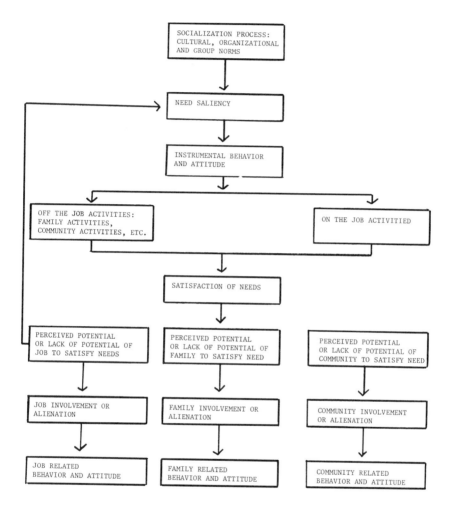

In the context of job involvement, individuals' beliefs that they are job involved or alienated depends on whether the job is perceived to have the potential for satisfying their salient needs. The saliency or the importance of different needs for individuals is determined by individuals' past experiences with groups of which they were members (socialization process) and with jobs that they have held. Different groups of people are influenced by different cultural, group, and organizational norms, and, thus, they tend to develop different needs structures or to set different goals and objectives for their lives. For example, the work-motivation literature suggests that the sources of job involvement for managers within any organization may be very different from those for unskilled laborers because of differences in the need saliencies of the two groups. Managers may value more autonomy and control in their jobs, whereas the unskilled laborers may attach greater importance to security and a sense of belonging in their jobs. Such value differences stem essentially from past socialization processes and from the influence of the norms of the groups to which the workers belong.

Some recent cross-cultural studies have demonstrated that because of the differences in the socialization process, workers belonging to different cultures differ with respect to the importance they attach to various job outcomes. The importance attached to various job outcomes reflects the saliency of the needs of workers. For instance, studies of Francophone and Anglophone managers in Canada (Kanungo 1977, 1980; Kanungo, Gorn, and Dauderis 1976) revealed that security and affiliation needs seem to have greater saliency for Francophone managers, whereas autonomy and achievement needs tend to have greater saliency for Anglophone managers. Similar results were reported in an international study (Kanungo and Wright 1981) that compared French managers in France with British managers in the United Kingdom. The salient needs tend to determine the central life interests of the individuals. On the job, the saliency of a need in individuals may be reinforced when they find that through job behavior they are capable of meeting their needs. Their perception that the job is capable of satisfying their important needs will make the individuals devote most of their available energy to the job. The workers will immerse themselves in the job, and the feedback from their job behavior will lead the workers to believe that the job is an essential part of themselves. They thus become job involved. If, however, the job is perceived by the individuals as lacking in opportunities for satisfying salient needs, they will develop a tendency to withdraw effort from the job and, thus, become alienated from it. For the satisfaction of their salient needs, the workers will redirect their energy elsewhere by engaging in various off-the-job activities or undesirable on-the-job activities.

Some recent comparative studies (Kanungo 1980) of job involvement among Francophone and Anglophone workers have provided indirect evidence in support of this motivational approach to job involvement. On the premise that Anglophone workers are a product of the Protestant-ethic socialization process and that they value job autonomy and achievement to a greater extent than Francophone workers, they are expected to show a greater psychological identification with their jobs than Francophone workers. Such a prediction is based on previous approaches to alienation that emphasize the importance of autonomy and control in the worker's self-concept. This prediction, however, was not confirmed by these studies. If anything, the results of these studies revealed stronger psychological job identification among Francophone workers than among Anglophone workers. The reason for greater job involvement among the Francophone workers may lie in the fact that they perceive their salient needs, such as security and affiliation tendencies, to be met to a greater extent on the job than do the Anglophone workers. Further empirical research is necessary, however, to test directly the implication of the motivational formulation in job situations.

The notion that job involvement has its roots both in the past socialization process and in the need-satisfying potential of the job environment seems to be supported by the work of several researchers (Rabinowitz and Hall 1977). For instance, psychology researchers (Blood and Hulin 1967; Hulin and Blood 1968; Lodahl 1964; Siegel 1969) who have studied job involvement as an individual-difference variable have proposed that job involvement has its roots in past socialization. Likewise, sociologists who have considered social structural and cultural variables (Goldthorpe et al. 1968; Weber 1930) to be important determinants of worker involvement have argued in favor of prior socialization being the root cause of job involvement. On the other hand, several psychologists (Argyris 1964; Bass 1965; McGregor 1960), who have studied involvement as a function of the job situation, and several sociologists (Blauner 1964), who have emphasized the important role of technology and structure of the organization in work alienation, have proposed that the root of involvement lies in the need-satisfying potential of the job environment. It is important, however, to keep in mind that the cognitive state of involvement is caused by both the socialization process and the job environment. Future studies should be directed toward assessing the relative contributions of each of these causes of job involvement.

Figure 6.1 also suggests that a cognitive state of job involvement will have a significant influence on job behavior and job attitudes. Several interesting possibilities present themselves in this regard. It would be worthwhile to investigate the influence of the state of involvement on the quality and intensity of job attitudes. Job involvement does not necessarily cause positive job attitudes but perhaps does affect the intensity of job attitudes. The effects of the state of involvement on the quality and quantity of job productivity and on membership behavior (turnover, absenteeism, tardiness, and so on) also need to be investigated in future research.

Conditions of Work Involvement

Involvement of individuals with work in general refers to the normative belief regarding how important work should be in their lives. It is the value or significance people attach to having work or performing work in general. It is the issue of how central working is in one's life when compared with other life roles (such as maintaining and raising a family or participating in the community). Viewed in this way, development of a cognitive belief state of identification with work in general would depend very much upon past and present socialization experiences. Individuals are trained through the influence of their culture and reference-group norms to believe in the centrality of work roles in life. Once formed, such beliefs are maintained through constant social support from reference groups and other forms of environmental reinforcements. Individuals learn to value work (or the goodness and morality of work) because of past parental, school, and religious training. They maintain their normative beliefs because of present socialization through reference-group support and favorable environmental conditions.

Training in the Protestant ethic in one's formative years can produce a normative belief in the goodness and centrality of work or work involvement. However, in later life, the normative belief state can weaken because of lack of opportunity for employment, easy access to unemployment benefits, war, and so on. For instance, during the era of the "flower children" in the 1960s, there was a decline in work involvement among U.S. middle-class youth and young adults. The decline in the work ethic resulted from the hostile environment created by the prospect of being killed in the Vietnam War and a lack of support from the social environment for the work ethic. The work ethic, which requires some degree of asceticism and self-discipline, could not thrive in a social environment that provided affluency and encouraged indulgence in total freedom.

It must be pointed out that socialization of the Protestant-ethic variety is not the only type of training that increases work involvement. Any type of training through which individuals realize that the centrality of the work role in life can fulfill their salient needs should increase work involvement. For instance, socialization in many Western cultures emphasizes individualism and promotes in its members greater saliency for autonomy and personal achievement needs. The Protestant work ethic in such cultures trains people to believe that work can satisfy these salient needs and can bring about a sense of individualism. Therefore, work should be valued as being good and central to one's life.

Socialization in many Eastern cultures, however, promotes in its members a sense of collectivism and saliency for social and security needs. In these cultures, religious preachings about achieving a universal brotherhood of mankind and religious practices advocating the value of sacrificing self-interest for the benefit of others have a different socializing influence. People in these cultures develop beliefs in the centrality of work not because work can promote personal achievement, but because work can fulfill the collectivistic goals of brotherhood and sharing in life. The Hindu religion, for example, encourages a form of work ethic that considers work as central to one's life, but it must be performed as a duty in the service of others (family members, friends, relatives, even strangers) and not for one's own personal achievement. Believing that work can bring about a sense of collectivism and also fulfill the salient social and security needs in one's life, a Hindu perhaps might show the same level of work involvement as a Protestant.

The case of Japan provides another example of a work ethic that can result from socialization training of a non-Protestant variety. The behavioral patterns and customs of the Japanese people have been deeply influenced by Confucianism, which stresses a rigid, hierarchically arranged collective society. Members of each collectivity are expected to maintain absolute loyalty and obedience to authority and to the group in the fulfillment of their obligations. In her classic work, Nakane (1970) distinguishes between the concepts of "frame" and "attribute," concluding that the Japanese tend to attach more importance to the frame (or the organizational situation within which the individual operates) than to the attributes or personal characteristics of the individual. Similarly, England and Lee (1974) concluded that "in view of this cultural background, it is not surprising that more successful Japanese managers place relatively greater emphasis upon 'loyalty' and relatively less emphasis upon 'me' than do managers in other countries" (p. 417). The influence of cultural and reference-group norms in Japan trains the Japanese to view work as a kind of sacred duty to be performed for a collective interest and not for a personal interest. As Aonuma (1981) explains, "The Japanese equivalent of the Protestant Ethic lies in the concept of sacrificing personal interest for organizational good. . . . Out of this ethic grew a sense of purpose regarding work—a concept of work not as drudgery, but as a kind of sacred duty. Work fulfills this duty, and thereby establishes a sense of purpose" (pp. 44–45). The above examples demonstrate that people belonging to different cultures tend to develop different salient needs influenced by different cultural and group norms. However, the socialization training in any given culture that emphasizes the instrumentality of work roles in satisfying peoples' culturally determined salient needs is primarily responsible for the development of work involvement.

Integration of the Sociological Approach

The sociological approach to work alienation can be adequately interpreted within the framework of the motivational approach. According to this framework, job and work alienation result primarily

TABLE 6.1

Integration of Sociological Approaches

Sociological Approach		Motivational Approach	
Types of Work Alienation	Environmental Conditions Responsible for Alienation	Personal Need Saliency of Worker	Perceived Work–Job Potential to Satisfy Salient Need
Isolation	Lack of social integration of worker	Affiliative-need saliency	Lack of a sense of membership
Normlessness	Breakdown of social norms	Self-evaluation(social comparison)-need saliency	Lack of information (norms) to guide behavior
Meaninglessness	Work simplification	Ego-need saliency	Lack of sense of responsibility
Powerlessness	Mechanization	Ego-need saliency	Lack of freedom (autonomy) and control (responsibility)
Self-estrangement	Lack of utilization of abilities or potentialities	Self-actualization- or achievement-need saliency	Lack of opportunity to utilize one's potentialities and lack of a sense of achievement

from a perceived lack of potential (in a job or in work in general) to satisfy the salient needs of the individual. The link between this framework and the sociological description of alienation is summarized in Table 6.1.

Sociologists (Blauner 1964; Seeman 1959) have described five different variants of work alienation: powerlessness, meaninglessness, normlessness, isolation, and self-estrangement. Each variant refers to a different, subjectively felt psychological state of an individual caused by different environmental conditions. If one describes these states in motivational terms, each variant represents a work situation that frustrates some salient needs of the individual. The isolation variant of job alienation will be experienced by individuals whose social and belonging needs are most salient and who find that their work situation does not have the potential to satisfy these needs. Blauner (1964) seems to concur with this position when he states that the state of isolation "implies the absence of a sense of membership in an industrial community" (p. 24). In Canada, the isolation type of job alienation has been reported more often among French Canadian workers than among English Canadian workers, perhaps because in the former case the necessary conditions for a state of isolation are present to a greater extent. Studies on the motivational orientation (Auclair and Read 1966) of French Canadian workers reveal that their affiliative needs (desire to belong to the industrial community) are salient, and yet such needs are frustrated because of the Anglophone ownership of industry. For very similar reasons, female workers may often experience a greater degree of isolation at work than male workers.

The normlessness variant of job alienation can be observed in persons who have a salient need for information to predict their physical and social job environment so that they can evaluate their present job behavior and plan future courses of action. For instance, workers with a salient need for feedback on how well they are doing may develop a feeling of normlessness in their jobs if the organization does not provide information on how performance is appraised and how rewards (merit pay, promotion, and so on) are administered. Workers may develop beliefs about the normlessness of work in general when they find that work organizations do not provide the necessary information about work. Workers with a high need for achievement (McClelland 1967) may have a stronger need for information than workers with a low need for achievement. Hence, the former type of worker may have a stronger tendency to develop beliefs about the normlessness of job or work than the latter group.

The meaninglessness variant of job alienation results from situations where the work process is broken down into simple minuscule tasks. Such job situations represent a high degree of job simplification, and for the worker they involve no real responsibility. Faced with such situations, the worker loses all sense of purpose and the job becomes meaningless. Translated into motivational terms, this implies that workers with a salient need for assuming a high degree of personal responsibility experience meaninglessness in their jobs when the need is frustrated because of job simplification or fragmentation. Workers with a high education, skill level, and need for achievement may have a stronger need for assuming personal responsibility than less-educated, unskilled, and low-need-for-achievement workers. Thus, the former categories of workers may be more susceptible to the meaninglessness variant of alienation when the job does not provide greater responsibility. Perhaps for similar reasons, the alienation of intellectuals toward work in general tends to be of the meaninglessness variety (Seeman 1959; Mills 1951).

Job alienation in the form of powerlessness refers to a perceived lack of control over one's work situation. According to Blauner (1964), the feeling of powerlessness on the job results from the mechanization process that controls the pace of work and limits workers' free movements. In motivational terms, the powerlessness type of alienation may be experienced by individuals who have salient ego needs, such as the need for autonomy, control, or self-esteem, but find the job environment incapable of satisfying them.

The final variant of alienation proposed by sociologists is self-estrangement at work. Blauner (1964) suggests that a job encourages self-estrangement if it does not provide an opportunity for expressing "unique abilities, potentialities, or personality of the worker" (p. 26). In motivational terms, such a state of alienation is experienced by people who have high self-actualization needs (Maslow 1954), such as the need for achievement, and find the job situation limiting the realization of their potential. Thus, from a motivational standpoint, the different types of job or work alienation suggested by sociologists represent the same cognitive belief of separation from job or work and are different from one another only in the sense that they are caused by a different saliency structure of needs in the individuals. The motivational reinterpretation of the sociological approach needs to be validated through empirical studies designed to test several predictions discussed above.

Some Major Differences between the
Present and Earlier Approaches

At this point, it may be useful to compare and to highlight a few important differences between the motivational approach and earlier ones. Although the definitions of job involvement and alienation as

cognitive states of identification with or separation from a job resemble the way the concepts were defined by Lawler and Hall (1970),
the former are different from the latter in one important respect.
As discussed earlier, Lawler and Hall put exclusive emphasis on the
job opportunities that meet a worker's need for control and autonomy
as necessary preconditions to the state of job involvement. In fact,
all earlier formulations (both sociological and psychological) seem to
have followed this line of thinking.

The motivational approach, however, suggests that job involvement does not necessarily depend on job characteristics that allow for
control- and autonomy-need satisfaction. It emphasizes that workers
have a variety of needs, some more salient than others. The saliency
of the needs in any given individual is determined by past socialization
in a given culture (historical causes) and is constantly modified by
present job conditions (contemporary causes). Different groups of
individuals, because of their different socialization training or different cultural background, may develop different need-saliency patterns. They may value extrinsic and intrinsic job outcomes (Lawler
1973) very differently. One set of needs (for example, growth needs,
such as self-esteem and autonomy) may be salient in one group of
workers, but the same needs may not be salient in another group.
This may result in different self-images in the two groups and, consequently, in different job expectations in the two groups. One group
of workers that considers control and autonomy to be the core of their
self-image may get involved in jobs that are perceived as offering an
opportunity for exercising control and autonomy, and they may become
alienated from jobs that are perceived as providing little freedom and
control. Such job characteristics, however, may not be the crucial
considerations for another group (who may view security and social
needs to be the core of their self-image) in the determination of their
job involvement or alienation. That people do differ with respect to
what constitutes the core of their self-concepts should not be over-
looked. The developed societies of the West may make their citizens
believe that all that counts in one's life is to have individual liberty
and freedom. Workers belonging to these societies may feel, therefore, that a working life is of little worth without freedom and control.
However, in the developing societies of the East, economic and social
security often are considered more important to life than are freedom
and control. Thus, workers in Eastern societies may find work very
involving if it guarantees such security, but may not care very much
for freedom and control in their jobs. In these societies, people may
value equality and sharing more than liberty and control as the guiding principle of a working life. Rabinowitz and Hall (1977) alluded to
this possibility but found no available research that examined "this
lower-need-based form of job involvement" (p. 280).

Earlier conceptualizations of work alienation and involvement confused alienation from a specific job with alienation from work in general. Such confusion primarily resulted from the emphasis on intrinsic motivation and the Protestant work ethic as the main source of work involvement. The present conceptualization, however, considers the work ethic as a normative belief in the goodness of work and distinguishes it from job involvement. A work ethic can result from socialization training of both Protestant and non-Protestant varieties. In the socialization process, any religious or cultural value that considers work as instrumental in satisfying culturally determined salient needs is capable of developing a work ethic in people. In individualistic societies, religious values, such as those found in Protestantism, characterize work as an important source of salient ego-need satisfaction and provide work with the moral character of being "good" and "desirable." In collectivistic societies, work also is characterized as "good" and "desirable" through the influence of religious values. However, in this case work is viewed as a source of satisfaction in life because it has the potentiality of fulfilling salient affiliative and security needs.

In their attempts to increase job involvement among workers, the sociological (Blauner 1964) and the psychological (Lawler and Hall 1970) approaches have analyzed the work situation from the standpoint of job design or the nature of the job. They have emphasized job characteristics, such as the lack of variety in a job, mechanized and routine operations, strict supervision, and so on, and their effects on the involvement of workers without any attempt to understand the nature and the saliency of needs in the workers. In presenting such a position, these authors have argued in favor of a universal prescription for increasing job involvement by designing jobs to provide greater autonomy and control to the workers. The prescription is, of course, based on the assumption that the needs for control and autonomy are the most salient needs in workers.

This position can be contrasted with the approach that Taylor (1911) advocated in his principles of scientific management. In his pig-iron-loading experiment, he selected as his subject a physically strong individual who had a salient monetary need. In selecting the right man for the job, he looked into the past training and abilities, the need saliency, and the job perceptions of the worker. Presumably, Taylor must have thought that these characteristics have a significant influence on a worker's job involvement. The approach advocated in the motivational formulation does not make the assumption that the needs for control and autonomy are the most salient needs in all workers. Unlike previous approaches, the present approach suggests that job involvement can best be understood if we find out the nature and the saliency of needs in workers as determined by prior socialization and present job conditions. The design of jobs and the determination of their extrinsic and intrinsic outcomes for the sake of increasing job involvement should be based on an understanding of workers needs and perceptions. The findings of Lawler and Hackman (1971) seem to support this position. According to them, "There is no reason to expect job changes to affect the motivation and satisfaction of employees who do not value the rewards that their jobs have to offer" (p. 52).

Previous approaches emphasized the distinction between work as an instrumental activity and work as consummatory activity (the means to an end versus the end in itself). The present approach considers work to be a set of job-related behaviors and attitudes, and like all behaviors and attitudes, work is considered to be instrumental in satisfying a variety of needs that a worker may have. All human behaviors stem from need states, and all human behaviors tend to be purposive and instrumental in obtaining goals or outcomes for the satisfaction of needs. Work behaviors and job attitudes should not be an exception to this rule.

In summary, the motivational approach to the study of alienation and involvement advocated in this chapter provides an integrative framework for future psychological and sociological research. Future research in the area should attempt not only to measure job and work alienation or involvement as cognitive states but should also attempt to relate such cognitive states to the antecedent conditions of need saliency in individuals and their job perceptions. Attempts should also be made to relate the cognitive states of alienation and involvement to the various affective states that accompany them and to their behavioral consequences. Using the motivational approach, future studies should explore the phenomena of alienation and involvement in areas other than job and work, such as in the family, in the community, and in other forms of leisure-time pursuits (as suggested in Figure 6.1). It would be of considerable interest to find out the reasons for alienation and involvement in these areas for different groups of people with different socialization training. It would also be of interest to see how involvement and alienation in one area influence the nature of such states in other areas. For instance, how does job involvement affect family involvement and vice versa? The widely accepted Marxian dictum that work alienation is the cause of all social maladies is something that clearly needs empirical verification. These are some of the general issues that need exploration in the future, and it is hoped that the framework proposed here will help in such exploration.

7

MEASUREMENT OF ALIENATION

While you and i have lips and voices which
are kissing and to sing with
who cares if some one-eyed son of a bitch
invents an instrument to measure Spring with?

                                        E. E. Cummings

INTRODUCTION

The investigation of any social phenomenon involves some theoretical or rational formulation regarding what the phenomenon is like. In social sciences, theoretical formulations require the development of scientific constructs that define the social phenomenon under study and describe its antecedent and consequent conditions. Once the constructs are developed in a theoretical framework, the next step is to operationalize the constructs so that the phenomenon represented by the constructs can be identified and measured with some degree of objectivity. In dealing with social phenomenon the problem of measurement of the constructs is as important as the rational formulations. Both the measurement of constructs and their rational formulation are mutually dependent on each other. In fact, as Warr, Cook, and Wall (1979) pointed out, "Adequate measurement of complex psychological states usually requires an iterative process; researchers must move several times between conceptualization and operationalization, adjusting their ideas and measures as they go" (p. 129).

Measurement is a device for standardization and quantification. Through measurement the social phenomena under study get their concrete identifiable shapes. Also through measurement the phenomena captured at different times and by different social scientists (using the same measuring instruments) can have equivalence. Through such equivalence and quantification, measurement can render more precise and reliable descriptions of the constructs and their antecedent and consequent conditions. Therefore, theoretical constructs representing the phenomena and their measurement go hand in hand. Constructs without measurements are vague and meaningless. Measurements without constructs are empty.

The above description of the nature of theoretical constructs and their measurement holds true for the study of involvement-alienation among workers. A theoretical reformulation called the motivational approach for the study of involvement with a "specific job" or "work in general" was developed and described in the previous chapter. Clearly, the motivational approach is in need of empirical verification. This requires operationalization of the constructs "job" and "work involvement" as described in the motivational approach. The present chapter describes a study that operationalizes the constructs. However, before describing the study, the problems with the existing measures of the constructs will be briefly reviewed. The reader may refer to Chapter 5 for a detailed discussion of such problems.

In the past, several instruments have been designed by sociologists and psychologists to measure involvement-alienation among workers. Most of these instruments, however, suffer from problems of construct validity. In order to illustrate the problems with existing measures, I have chosen five of the more recently developed, psychometrically acceptable, and widely used instruments (items from these instruments are presented in Appendix A). Two of the instruments (Lodahl and Kejner 1965; Saleh and Hosek 1976) were specifically designed to measure job involvement. Two other instruments (Blood 1969; Warr, Cook, and Wall 1979) were designed to measure involvement with work in general. Blood considered the notions of work involvement (as opposed to specific job involvement) and the Protestant work ethic to be equivalent, and such equivalence is reflected in his measure. Warr, Cook, and Wall, in developing their measure of work involvement, defined the construct as "the extent to which a person wants to be engaged in work." The fifth instrument was designed by Shepard (1971) to measure five varieties of work alienation suggested by sociologists (Seeman 1959).

The problems of construct validity for each of these measures stem from the fact that the items in these instruments are measuring constructs that carry excess meaning. Four of these instruments contain items that reflect not only workers' involvement as a state of psychological identification but also states of their intrinsic motivation. The job-involvement scale developed by Lodahl and Kejner contains items, such as "I live, eat and breathe my job," representing a person's psychological identification with the job. It also contains other items, such as "Sometimes I'd like to kick myself for the mistakes I make in my work," representing a person's intrinsic motivation for fulfilling self-esteem needs at work. Likewise, Blood's measure of work involvement or the Protestant work ethic includes both involvement and intrinsic-motivation items. For instance, an item like "Wasting time is as bad as wasting money" represents the greater importance or centrality of work in one's life. But the item "If all other things are equal, it is better to have a job with a lot of responsibility than one with little responsibility" clearly reflects intrinsic motivation. Agreement with the item implies a person's strong desire to fulfill the need for responsibility. Among all the instruments developed so far, only the most recent one (Warr, Cook, and Wall) seems to have excluded intrinsic-motivation items. As was pointed out in Chapter 5, the inclusion of intrinsic-motivation items in instruments designed to measure job and work involvement creates an artifact showing that involvement is positively related to intrinsic-need strength and intrinsic-job outcomes.

It may also be pointed out that items in all the five instruments have used the constructs of "job" and "work" in an interchangeable manner, creating further problems of construct validity. The distinction between job and work involvement suggested by the motivational approach not only puts the two constructs in a specific-general dimension but also considers the two constructs to be operating at two different levels: descriptive and normative. Job involvement, according to the motivational approach, is a descriptive positive belief about a specific job, whereas work involvement is a normative belief regarding the value of the work role in life. Conventional morality in a society may teach an individual to value very highly work roles in life and, consequently, to consider work as being more desirable than being idle or unemployed. However, such a normative belief may not necessarily create high involvement in one's present job. Conversely, a person highly involved in a present job may not necessarily attach positive moral values to work in general. The descriptive belief regarding involvement in one's job and the normative belief regarding the value of work in one's life are two conceptually distinct notions. Combining items reflecting the two types of beliefs into a single measuring instrument can only provide misleading and hard-to-interpret information.

Furthermore, in the past, researchers have confused the issue of identifying the antecedent conditions of worker's involvement with the issue of identifying the state of job involvement and its subsequent effects. Saleh and Hosek's (1976) scale, for instance, contains three categories of items that describe the presumed causal conditions of job involvement (for example, "How much chance do you get to do things your own way?"); the presumed effects of job involvement (for example, "I avoid taking on extra duties and responsibilities in my work"); and the state of job involvement itself (for example, "The most important things I do are involved with my job"). Finally, these instruments include items that describe the construct of involvement as both a cognitive and a positive emotional state of the worker. Lodahl and Kejner's (1965) scale contains items that represent these two meanings. Items such as "The major satisfaction in my life comes from my job" and "The most important things that happen to me involve my work" are descriptions of affective and cognitive states, respectively.

In view of the above construct-validity problems associated with the existing instruments, the constructs of job and work involvement as defined by the motivational approach cannot be measured by them. According to the motivational approach, involvement either in the context of a particular job or with work in general can be viewed as a unidimensional cognitive or belief state of psychological identification. An individual's psychological identification with a particular job (or with work in general) depends on the saliency of the person's needs (both extrinsic and intrinsic) and the perceptions the person has about the need-satisfying potentialities of the job (or work). Viewed in this way, job involvement and work involvement cannot be reflected accurately when measured by existing instruments. This necessitates the development of valid and reliable new measures of job and work involvement for use in future research. The following section describes a study that developed some new measures of the concepts.

METHOD

Item Construction for Involvement Scales

The study was designed to develop scale items that reflected only an individual's cognitive state of psychological identification with a specific job and with work in general. Furthermore, these items can take different forms, such as a statement in a questionnaire requiring agreement or disagreement from the individual or a pictorial or graphic item representing varying degrees of psychological identification. In the present study, for the purpose of measuring involvement with each of the two distinct contexts (specific job and general work), three different measurement formats—questionnaire, semantic differential (Osgood, Suci, and Tannenbaum 1957), and graphic techniques—were selected. Questionnaire items that directly reflected a cognitive state of psychological identification were judged and compiled by 10 graduate students after a thorough search of the existing measures of involvement and alienation in both the psychological and sociological literature (Blauner 1964; Blood 1969; Clark 1959; Dubin 1956; Lodahl and Kejner 1965; Saleh and Hosek 1976; Wollack et al.

TABLE 7.1

Job- and Work-Involvement Scale Items

	Mean	Standard Deviation	Item-Total Correlation
Job-Involvement Scales			
Semantic-differential format (JISD scale)			
To me my present job is:			
1. Involving/noninvolving	2.99	1.70	0.77
2. Important/unimportant	2.89	1.59	0.77
3. Fundamental/trivial	3.22	1.46	0.65
4. Essential/nonessential	3.04	1.61	0.69
In relation to my present job I am:			
5. Identified/not identified	2.89	1.75	0.79
6. Attached/detached	3.23	1.72	0.82
7. Integrated/nonintegrated	3.13	1.51	0.64
8. United/disunited	3.38	1.51	0.73
JISD scale (8 items)	23.94	10.07	—
Questionnaire format (JIQ scale)			
1. The most important things that happen to me involve my present job	3.23	1.35	0.72
2. To me, my job is only a small part of who I am	3.32	1.54	0.68
3. I am very much involved personally in my job	3.94	1.40	0.68
4. I live, eat, and breathe my job	2.18	1.34	0.63
5. Most of my interests are centered around my job	2.68	1.31	0.74
6. I have very strong ties with my present job which would be very difficult to break	3.14	1.48	0.68
7. Usually I feel detached from my job	4.03	1.40	0.59
8. Most of my personal life goals are job-oriented	3.35	1.41	0.62
9. I consider my job to be very central to my existence	3.15	1.42	0.73
10. I like to be absorbed in my job most of the time	3.32	1.41	0.63
JIQ scale (10 items)	31.31	10.61	—
Graphic format (JIG scale)			
1. Overlapping circles	4.25	1.45	0.70
2. Person and desk	4.35	1.54	0.70
JIG scale (2 items)	8.39	3.01	—

	Mean	Standard Deviation	Item-Total Correlation
Work-Involvement Scales			
Semantic–differential format (WISD scale)			
To me work in general is:			
1. Involving/noninvolving	2.36	1.21	0.73
2. Important/unimportant	2.18	1.12	0.76
3. Fundamental/trivial	2.71	1.29	0.71
4. Essential/nonessential	2.48	1.41	0.72
In relation to work in general I am:			
5. Identified/not identified	2.56	1.29	0.78
6. Attached/detached	2.70	1.20	0.82
7. Integrated/nonintegrated	2.99	1.39	0.73
8. United/disunited	2.98	1.33	0.75
WISD scale (8 items)	20.30	8.28	—
Questionnaire format (WIQ scale)			
1. The most important things that happen in life involve work	3.64	1.22	0.68
2. Work is something people should get involved in most of the time	3.71	1.22	0.65
3. Work should be only a small part of one's life	3.91	1.17	0.54
4. Work should be considered central to life	3.69	1.18	0.70
5. In my view, an individual's personal life goals should be work-oriented	3.40	1.16	0.74
6. Life is worth living only when people get absorbed in work	3.02	1.28	0.66
WIQ scale (6 items)	20.70	5.97	—
Graphic format (WIG scale)			
1. Overlapping circle	4.51	1.37	0.68
2. Person and desk	4.53	1.56	0.68
WIG scale (2 items)	9.04	2.69	—

Note: Item scores are based on responses from 703 respondents. On semantic-differential items lower scores mean higher involvement. In all other cases, higher scores mean higher involvement.

1971). There was complete agreement by the 10 judges on 12 items for inclusion in the Job Involvement Questionnaire scale (JIQ) and on 9 items for inclusion in the Work Involvement Questionnaire scale (WIQ). For the JIQ and WIQ items, six-point, agree-disagree response formats were used. Subsequent item analyses resulted in dropping two items from the JIQ and three items from the WIQ scales because of their low interitem and item-total correlations. Thus, the final scales contained ten and six items, respectively. These items are presented in Table 7.1 (they also appear in Appendix B).

Another six graduate students made an extensive search for key words that clearly reflected the notion of psychological identification using available literature and dictionaries for synonyms and antonyms. This process yielded 11 bipolar items on which all the six judges agreed. These items were used to construct a Job Involvement Semantic Differential (JISD) scale and a Work Involvement Semantic Differential (WISD) scale. These semantic differential items used seven-point response formats. Subsequent item analyses led to eliminating three items from each of the two scales, again on the basis of interitem and item-total correlations. Thus, each scale contained eight items, and these are also presented in Table 7.2 (they also appear in Appendix B). Both the questionnaire and semantic-differential scales used five and four filler items, respectively, in order to reduce the demand characteristics of the scale items designed to measure a single construct.

Finally, three graphic items representing the notion of psychological identification were prepared for use in each of the job and work contexts. Two of these items were finally selected after item analyses. (These graphic items as they appeared in the questionnaire are presented in Appendix B.) The two items—overlapping circles and person–desk relationship—designed to measure job involvement constituted the Job Involvement Graphic scale (JIG). Likewise, the two items designed to measure work involvement constituted the Work Involvement Graphic scale (WIG). Both JIG and WIG items used a seven-point response format.

Design of the Questionnaire

A questionnaire containing three parts was designed for the purpose of testing the reliability and validity of the newly constructed job- and work-involvement scales. Part I of the questionnaire contained only items that assessed respondents' views on the value of their present job in their lives. Thus, this part of the questionnaire included JISD, JIQ, and JIG scale items. In addition, this part included two other instruments. One instrument measured the perceived importance of 15 job outcomes by asking the respondents to rank them, the other measured on a six-point scale the respondents' satisfaction with the same 15 job outcomes and their overall satisfaction with their present job. The 15 job outcomes included eight organizationally controlled rewards (comfortable working conditions, restricted hours of work, adequate earnings, fair pay, sound company policy, job security, benefits, and promotion opportunities); four interpersonally mediated rewards (considerate supervision, competent technical supervision, good interpersonal relations, and respect and recognition from others); and three internally mediated rewards (responsibility and independence, achievement, and interesting nature of work). The validity and reliability of these two instruments have been established in earlier studies (Gorn and Kanungo 1980; Kanungo, Gorn, and Dauderis 1976), and the instruments were used to test the criterion-related concurrent validity of the newly developed involvement scales. This part of the questionnaire was arranged in a way that separated the three job-involvement scales from each other by putting job-outcome-importance and job-satisfaction instruments in the middle.

Part II of the questionnaire contained items that assessed respondents' normative beliefs regarding the value of work in general in life without reference to any specific job. Thus, this part included the three work-involvement scales: WISD, WIQ, and WIG. Part Three of the questionnaire was designed to determine the demographic characteristics of the respondents.

The questionnaire described above was written in both French and English. The equivalence of the French and English versions of the questionnaire was established through the use of a translation-retranslation procedure. (The English version of the questionnaire is presented in Appendix B.)

Sample and Procedure

Earlier studies designed to develop instruments to measure job involvement have been criticized for their use of samples restricted to a very narrow range of job categories. For instance, the most widely used Lodahl and Kejner (1965) scale of job involvement was based on samples drawn from only two job categories (nurses and engineers). Likewise, the more recent Saleh and Hosek (1976) scale of job involvement was based on samples drawn from the sales department of an insurance company (sales managers and sales representatives). Psychometric properties of involvement scales derived from the use of one or two job categories have only limited value. Such scales may not provide an accurate index of job involvement for workers belonging to job categories very different from those used in the original studies. Studies dealing with the development of instruments should use highly heterogeneous samples so that the instruments can have wider applicability.

In order to get a very heterogeneous sample for the present study, it was decided to conduct the survey on 900 full-time employees enrolled in undergraduate and graduate-level evening extension courses offered in three major universities in Montreal. A large number of public and private sector organizations are located in and around Montreal. Employees from these organizations belonging to various job categories come to take the evening extension courses in the two English and one French university in Montreal. Many of these employees come to take professional courses for their career development, and many others come to take nonprofessional courses either for their own interest or to meet organizational requirements, such as competency in a second language.

The respondents were told that participation in the study was optional and that they could be assured of the confidentiality of the data. The respondents were asked not to put their names on the questionnaire and were requested to complete the questionnaire during the class hour in groups of varying sizes ranging from 40 to 100. The final count revealed that a total of 703 completed questionnaires were returned.

A separate, but parallel, study was conducted in two of the universities for assessing the test-retest reliabilities of the questionnaire. In each university, one evening extension course with approximately 50 full-time employees enrolled in it was used for the purpose. The participants in the course were administered the questionnaire or tested twice during the class hour, with a three-week interval between the first and second test. Each time the respondents were requested to put their student identification number on the front page of the questionnaire. During the first test, however, the respondents were not told that they would be tested again on the same questionnaire. The matching of identification numbers for the test and retest revealed that the data from 63 respondents could be used for the test-retest analysis.

RESULTS

Demographic Data

The demographic characteristics of the respondents presented in Table 7.2 reveal that the sample was quite heterogeneous in its composition. Employees belonging to public and private sector organizations were equally represented in the sample. Almost half of

TABLE 7.2

Demographic Characteristics of 703 Respondents

	Percent
Sex	
Male	56.8
Female	43.2
Age	
Less than 20	1.2
20-29	63.4
30-39	28.8
40-49	5.3
Greater than 50	1.3
Marital status	
Married	39.8
Single	60.2
Mother tongue	
French	36.6
English	41.0
Both	2.6
Other	19.8
Education	
Some high school	2.8
High school graduate	13.3
Some college	28.6
College degree	22.1
Some graduate study	19.4
Advanced degree	13.8
Employment sector	
Public	50.1
Private	49.9
Organization size (number of employees)	
Less than 200	29.6
200-700	17.9
Greater than 700	52.5
Years of organizational tenure	
Less than 2 years	19.7
2-5 years	48.7
6-10 years	20.4
11 years or more	11.2
Salary (dollars)	
Less than 10,000	12.3
10,000-19,999	56.0
20,000-29,999	25.2
30,000-39,999	5.1
Greater than 40,000	1.4

the employees came from large organizations (with more than 700
employees), and the other half came from small or medium-size organizations. Of the respondents, 57 percent were male and 43 percent were female, with a mean age of 28 years (standard deviation =
6.66) for the total sample. They were 37 percent French Canadian
and 41 percent English Canadian; the rest belonged to other ethnic
groups. Of the respondents, 40 percent were married and 60 percent
were single. Their education levels ranged from high school to an
advanced graduate degree, and their income levels ranged from less
than $10,000 a year to more than $40,000 per year. Almost half the
sample had organizational tenure of from two to five years. From the
other half of the sample, approximately 20 percent had less than two
years and 30 percent had more than five years of organizational experience. These respondents came from 16 different job categories
(accounting, civil service, computer programming and system analysis, computer operations, education, engineering, health profes-
sions, labor and public relations, management, personnel, production, purchasing, research, sales, secretarial, and transportation).

Empirical Properties of the Involvement Scales

Item Analyses

Separate item analyses of 11 items initially included in JISD
and WISD measures resulted in a decision to eliminate 3 items
that gave rise to relatively low item-total correlations (ranging from
0.35 to 0.50). The remaining eight items were included in the final
scales, and the mean, standard deviation, and item-total correlations
for each item are presented in Table 7.1. Separate item analyses of
12 JIQ and 9 WIQ items revealed low item-total correlations (ranging from 0.12 to 0.49) for 2 items in JIQ scales and 3 items in
WIQ scales. The mean, standard deviation, and item-total correlations for the final 10 items in JIQ scale and 6 items in WIQ scale are
presented in Table 7.1. The table also presents means, standard
deviations, and intercorrelations for items in JIG and WIG scales.
Besides these item statistics, the table presents the means and standard deviations for each of the six involvement scales. It must be
pointed out that for JISD and WISD scales the scores range from 8.0
to 56.0; lower scores represent a higher involvement. For JIQ and
WIQ scales the scores range from 10.0 to 60.0 and 6.0 to 36.0, respectively; higher scores represent a higher involvement. Finally,
for JIG and WIG scales, the scores range from 2.0 to 14.0; higher
scores represent a higher involvement.

Reliabilities of the Scales

The internal-consistency reliabilities of the six involvement scales and the 15-item job-satisfaction scale used in the study are presented in Table 7.3. The reliability coefficients of the scales range from .68 to .89. Also included in the table are the test-retest reliability coefficients for each of the scales based on a separate sample of 63 respondents, who were administered the questionnaire twice within a three-week interval. The demographic characteristics of this sample are presented in Table 7.4. A comparison of the data in Table 7.4 with the data in Table 7.1 shows that the sample of 63 respondents used in the test-retest study is not very different from the main sample of 703 respondents. The test-retest reliability coefficients of the scales shown in Table 7.3 range from .67 to .87. Data in Table 7.3 clearly suggest that both the reliability of the repeated measurements and of the internal consistency of items are adequate for these scales.

TABLE 7.3

Reliability Coefficients for Involvement and Job–Satisfaction Scales

	Internal Consistency Coefficient	Test-Retest Coefficient
Job involvement		
Semantic differential (JISD scale)	.81	.74
Questionnaire (JIQ scale)	.87	.85
Graphic (JIG scale)	.70	.82
Work involvement		
Semantic differential (WISD scale)	.83	.78
Questionnaire (WIQ scale)	.75	.67
Graphic (WIG scale)	.68	.67
Job satisfaction		
15-item scale	.89	.73
Overall job satisfaction (single item)	—	.87

Note: Internal Consistency (Cronbach alpha) coefficients are based on data from 703 respondents. Test-retest coefficients are based on data from 63 respondents.

TABLE 7.4

Demographic Characteristics of Test-Retest Sample
(63 respondents)

	Percent
Sex	
Male	48.4
Female	51.6
Age	
20-29	58.1
30-39	37.1
40-49	3.2
Greater than 50	1.6
Marital status	
Married	46.8
Single	53.2
Mother tongue	
French	27.4
English	50.0
Both	1.6
Other	21.0
Education	
Some high school	3.2
High school graduation	21.0
Some college	30.6
College degree	24.2
Some graduate study	17.7
Advanced degree	3.2
Employment sector	
Public	59.0
Private	41.0
Organization size (number of employees)	
Less than 200	27.9
200-700	11.5
Greater than 700	60.7
Years of organizational tenure	
Less than 2 years	11.3
2-5 years	54.8
6-10 years	22.6
11 years or more	11.3
Salary (dollars)	
Less than 10,000	9.8
10,000-19,999	45.9
20,000-29,999	37.7
30,000-39,999	4.9
Greater than 40,000	1.6

Convergent and Discriminant Validity
of Involvement Scales

The convergent and discriminant validity of the job- and work-involvement measures were tested by comparing the median values of the off-diagonal correlations among scale items under three conditions: monotrait-heteromethod, heterotrait-monomethod, and heterotrait-heteromethod (Campbell and Fiske 1959). The results are presented in Table 7.5. It may be recalled that the study used three methods (semantic differential format, questionnaire format, and graphic format) to measure two traits (job and work involvement).

TABLE 7.5

Median Values of Strength of Association among Involvement-Scale Items

	Median r	Total Number of Correlations
Monotrait-Heteromethod		
JISD with JIQ and JIG scale items	.30	96
JIQ with JISD and JIG scale items	.30	100
JIG with JISD and JIQ scale items	.50	36
WISD with WIQ and WIG scale items	.30	64
WIQ with WISD and WIG scale items	.24	60
WIG with WISD and WIQ scale items	.40	20
Heterotrait-Monomethod		
JISD with WISD scale items	.14	64
JIQ with WIQ scale items	.17	60
JIG with WIG scale items	.24	4
Heterotrait-Heteromethod		
JISD with WIQ and WIG scale items	.04	64
JIQ with WISD and WIG scale items	.09	100
JIG with WISD and WIQ scale items	.13	28
WISD with JIQ and JIG scale items	.10	96
WIQ with JISD and JIG scale items	.04	60
WIG with JISD and JIQ scale items	.11	36

Note: Correlations greater than .10 are significant at the .01 level.

TABLE 7.6

Multitrait–Multimethod Matrix for Job– and Work–Involvement Scales
(N = 703)

	Semantic Differential		Questionnaire		Graphic	
	Job Involvement (JISD)	Work Involvement (WISD)	Job Involvement (JIQ)	Work Involvement (WIQ)	Job Involvement (JIG)	Work Involvement (WIG)
Semantic-differential format						
Job involvement (JISD)						
Work involvement (WISD)	$.28^a$					
Questionnaire format						
Job involvement (JIQ)	$-.33^b$	$.08^c$				
Work involvement (WIQ)	$.01^c$	$-.12^b$	$.29^a$			
Graphic format						
Job involvement (JIG)	$-.44^b$	$.09^c$	$.80^b$	$.21^c$		
Work involvement (WIG)	$.02^c$	$-.24$	$.33^c$	$.69^b$	$.36^a$	

[a] Represents heterotrait–monomethod values.
[b] Represents validity diagonal or monotrait–heteromethod values.
[c] Represents heterotrait–heteromethod values.

Note: Correlations greater than .11 are significant at the .01 level of confidence. Negative correlations are owing to the reverse scoring of scales using semantic-differential format.

It is expected that items measuring the same trait but using different methods (monotrait-heteromethod) should have a stronger association than items measuring different traits using the same method (mono-method-heterotrait). The weakest associations would exist among items measuring different traits using different methods (heterotrait-heteromethod). Results in Table 7.5 confirm these expectations and suggest that the convergent and discriminant validity of the scale items are satisfactory.

Analyses of median values of correlations among individual items on the six scales (as presented in Table 7.5) provide only a very general picture of convergent and discriminant validities. A more precise description of validities on the scales can be derived from a validational matrix suggested by Campbell and Fiske (1959). Such a matrix is presented in Table 7.6, showing the intercorrelations among the six involvement scales. From the validity diagonals (circled correlations in Table 7.6), it may be noticed that all the correlations are statistically significant (p $<$ .01), suggesting the convergent validity of the scales. However, the magnitude of the correlations suggests that the convergent validities of the questionnaire and graphic scales measuring job involvement (r = .80) and work involvement (r = .69) are quite high. By comparison, semantic-differential scales show a moderate to very weak relationship with other scales measuring job involvement or work involvement. The JISD scale shows a moderate relationship with both JIQ (r = -.33) and JIG (r = -.44) scales. The WISD scale shows a very weak relationship to both WIQ (r = .12) and WIG (r = -.24) scales.

Assessment of discriminant validities requires that monotrait-heteromethod values (agreement between different ways of measuring the same trait) should exceed the heterotrait-heteromethod values (agreement between different traits measured in different ways). The results in Table 7.6 show that every circled correlation representing a monotrait-heteromethod value is higher than the adjacent noncircled correlations representing the heterotrait-heteromethod value.

A second but more stringent criterion for the assessment of discriminant validity requires that monotrait-heteromethod values should exceed heterotrait-monomethod values (agreement between different traits measured the same way). This would indicate whether common-trait variance is greater than common-method variance. This criterion is satisfied in 67 percent of the cases. A closer inspection of Table 7.6 reveals that the semantic-differential format, particularly WISD measuring work involvement, does not meet this criterion. The validity of the WISD scale is questionable because the correlations between WISD and the other two work-involvement measures (r_s = -.12 and -.24) do not exceed the correlations between WISD and JISD (r = .28). In the case of the JISD scale, on the other hand, the validity criterion is met because the correlation between JISD and the two other job-involvement scales (r_s = -.33 and -.44) is higher than the correlation between JISD and WISD (r = .28). However, because of the moderate relationship of JISD to the other two job-involvement measures, its use should be discouraged.

The convergent and discriminant validities of the questionnaire and graphic scales seem to be quite adequate. In fact, if one removes the two semantic-differential scales (JISD and WISD) from the matrix in Table 7.6, the picture becomes quite clear. For the two job-involvement scales (JIQ and JIG) and the two work-involvement scales (WIQ and WIG), the monotrait-heteromethod correlations are .80 and .69, respectively. These are substantially higher than monomethod-heterotrait correlations of .36 and .29 and heteromethod-heterotrait correlations of .33 and .21.

The multitrait and multimethod matrix presented in Table 7.6 was further reanalyzed for confirmation using an analysis-of-variance, three-way classification model suggested by Kavanagh, Mackinney, and Wolins (1971). In this model, individual respondents are treated as random effects and traits and methods are treated as fixed effects. The purpose of this analysis is to estimate the three effects: respondent (R) effect (the degree to which the alternative methods and traits yield similar involvement scores or agreement within respondents); respondent X trait (RXT) interaction effect (the degree of rated discriminations on traits by respondents); and respondent X method (RXM) interaction effect (the degree of disagreement on methods by respondents). The first effect corresponds to an overall estimate of convergent validity. The second effect corresponds to an estimate of discriminant validity. The third effect corresponds to method bias. The results of the analysis of variance are presented in Table 7.7. Both the main effect of R and the RXT interaction effect are statistically significant (p < .01), suggesting confirmatory evidence for convergent and discriminant validities of the instruments.

Following the suggestion of Kavanagh, Mackinney, and Wolins, variance component (VC) and variance-component indexes for each of the three effects were also calculated to compare their relative impacts on the study. The results are also presented in Table 7.7. Although the RXM interaction (method bias) effect was not statistically significant, its variance-component index shows that its relative impact was not too small. The reason for this lies in the fact that the use of semantic-differential formats revealed some weaknesses. Separate estimations of variance components and variance-component indexes for matrixes with and without semantic-differential scales are presented in Table 7.8. The results in Table 7.8 clearly suggest that method bias and error components are substantially reduced

TABLE 7.7

Analysis of Variance of Multitrait-Multimethod Matrix

Source	df	MS	F	Variance Component	Variance-Component Index
Respondents (R)	702	2.94	4.45*	.33	.46
Respondents X trait (RXT)	702	.78	1.18*	.31	.44
Respondents X method (RXM)	1,404	.48	.72	.19	.33
Error	1,404	.66		.38	

*p < .01.

TABLE 7.8

Comparison of Methods Used to Measure Involvement

Source	Semantic Differential and Questionnaire		Semantic Differential and Graphic		Questionnaire and Graphic	
	Variance Component	Variance-Component Index	Variance Component	Variance-Component Index	Variance Component	Variance-Component Index
Respondents (R)	.25	.32	.33	.45	.53	.71
Respondents X trait (RXT)	.18	.26	.29	.42	.44	.67
Respondents X method (RXM)	.24	.32	.27	.40	.05	.19
Error	.51		.39		.21	

111

and the convergence and discriminant validities are clearly enhanced when semantic-differential scales are eliminated from the matrix.

Dimensionality of the Scales

Earlier in the chapter it was argued that, in order to avoid the problems of excess meaning, job- and work-involvement phenomena must be conceptualized in terms of unidimensional constructs. The motivational approach to involvement discussed in the previous chapter defined the phenomena in an unidimensional fashion by emphasiz-

TABLE 7.9

Factor Loadings on Job- and Work-Involvement Semantic-Differential Items

Scale Items	Factor Loadings	
	Factor 1	Factor 2
JISD		
1	.01	.73
2	.05	.63
3	.11	.42
4	.11	.46
5	.10	.79
6	.11	.82
7	.15	.58
8	.13	.69
WISD		
1	.69	.09
2	.75	.04
3	.66	-.02
4	.65	.04
5	.74	.15
6	.81	.10
7	.64	.15
8	.70	.16
Eigenvalue	5.19	2.97
Percent of variance explained	59.4	33.9

TABLE 7.10

Factor Loadings on Job- and Work-Involvement Questionnaire Items

Scale Items	Factor Loadings	
	Factor 1	Factor 2
JIQ		
1	.66	.17
2	.52	.00
3	.53	.02
4	.60	.14
5	.77	.18
6	.65	.03
7	.44	-.13
8	.53	.31
9	.66	.19
10	.50	.20
WIQ		
1	.18	.65
2	.11	.52
3	.07	.40
4	.10	.61
5	.10	.73
6	.11	.54
Eigenvalue	4.61	1.82
Percent of variance explained	67.1	26.5

ing only the dimension of psychological identification or separation of an individual in the job and work contexts. Any scale developed to measure the phenomena, therefore, must demonstrate their unidimensionality.

In order to find out whether the items in each of the six involvement scales measure a single dimension, the scores on job- and work-involvement items were factor analyzed separately for each of the three methods (semantic differential, questionnaire, and graphic). The principal-component analysis followed by a varimax rotation was used to arrive at factor solutions. The factor loadings on scale items are presented in Tables 7.9, 7.10, and 7.11. Each analysis yielded

TABLE 7.11

Factor Loadings on Job and Work-Involvement Graphic Items

Scale Items	Factor Loadings	
	Factor 1	Factor 2
JIG		
1	.95	.09
2	.70	.19
WIG		
1	.21	.70
2	.06	.89
Eigenvalue	1.81	.96
Percent of variance explained	65.3	34.7

two clear interpretable factors of job and work involvement. For semantic-differential (JISD and WISD items, the first factor loaded highly on WISD items (item loadings ranged from .64 to .81 for WISD and from .12 to .16 for JISD) and the second factor loaded highly on JISD items (item loadings ranged from .42 to .82 for JISD and from .02 to .15 for WISD). Eigenvalues for the two factors were 5.19 and 2.97, respectively, explaining 93.3 percent of the common variance. For questionnaire items, the first factor reflected job involvement (item loadings ranged from .44 to .77 for JIQ and from .07 to .18 for WIQ), and the second factor reflected work involvement (item loadings ranged from .40 to .73 for WIQ and from .00 to .31 for JIQ). The eigenvalues were 4.61 and 1.82, respectively, explaining 93.6 percent of the common variance. Finally, for the graphic items, job and work involvement emerged quite clearly as the first factor (item loadings were .95 and .70 for JIG and .09 and .19 for WIG) and the second factor (item loadings were .70 and .89 for WIG and .21 and .06 for JIG), respectively. The eigenvalues were 1.81 and 0.96, respectively, explaining 100 percent of the common variance. In addition to the three separate factor analyses, one final factor analysis was performed on the entire set of data (all items from all of the six involvement scales). Since the three separate factor analyses resulted in two clearly interpretable factors of job and work involvement, a two-factor solution was sought in the final factor analysis. The principal-component analysis followed by a varimax rotation was used to arrive at the fac-

TABLE 7.12

Factor Loading in a Two-Factor Solution for Items in All Six Scales

Scale Items	Factor Loadings	
	Factor 1	Factor 2
JISD		
1	.72	.00
2	.69	.04
3	.52	.06
4	.51	.07
5	.68	.03
6	.77	.06
7	.50	.10
8	.61	.08
JIQ		
1	.62	.15
2	.63	.10
3	.68	.10
4	.45	.12
5	.58	.13
6	.62	.03
7	.63	.07
8	.40	.25
9	.57	.19
10	.49	.20
JIG		
1	.79	.10
2	.79	.11
WISD		
1	.09	.65
2	.06	.71
3	.07	.60
4	.11	.57
5	.13	.68
6	.12	.79
7	.13	.57
8	.11	.64
WIQ		
1	.03	.51
2	.14	.45
3	..11	.48
4	.04	.46
5	.04	.48
6	.04	.34
WIG		
1	.13	.68
2	.07	.65
Eigenvalue	9.10	4.60
Percent of variance explained	66.4	33.6

tor solutions. Table 7.12 presents the factor loadings. In spite of
the introduction of method variance into this factor analysis, the first
factor has the highest loadings on job-involvement items, and the
second factor has the highest loadings on work-involvement items.
The results in Tables 7.9, 7.10, 7.11, and 7.12 clearly suggest that
not only job and work involvement operationalized by the scales used
in the study are distinct constructs, but also the items in each of the
job- and work-involvement scales are measuring a single belief dimension of psychological identification or separation.

SUMMARY AND CONCLUSION

The results presented in the previous section reveal that all
three job-involvement scales and two of the work-involvement scales
(WIQ and WIG) have satisfactory psychometric properties. The
scales have reasonable levels of internal consistency and test-retest
reliability. They seem to pass the tests of both convergent and discriminant validity. The job-involvement scale items seem to measure
unidimensional constructs of psychological identification (involvement)
or separation (alienation) in the job context. Likewise, the work-involvement scale items seem to measure unidimensional normative
beliefs about one's identification or separation in the general work
context.

Development of job- and work-involvement scales in this study
are based on the conceptual distinction between the two constructs as
proposed in the motivational approach. Compared with earlier measures of job involvement (Lodahl and Kejner 1965) and work involvement (Blood 1969), the new scales provide refinements in the definition and measurement of involvement in both the job and work contexts. Job and work involvement in these measures refer to two distinct sets of beliefs, which differ not only in terms of particular (job)
and general (work) contexts but also in terms of descriptive (job) and
normative (work) levels of operation. Such a distinction implies that
job involvement measured by the new scales is a descriptive belief
about one's relationship (identity with or separation from) to the
present job and is more a function of the perceived potentiality of the
job to satisfy one's salient needs. On the other hand, work involvement measured by the new scales refers to a normative belief about
the work role in life (code of ethic about work in general) and is more
a function of past socialization.

This study explored the use of three different formats for measuring job and work involvement. Previous researchers have mainly
used the questionnaire format. But for cross-cultural and comparative research, the use of other formats, such as graphic or pictorial

techniques, may be more effective (Kanungo 1979). Results of the study show that the two graphic scales (JIG and WIG) correlate highly with their respective questionnaire scales (JIQ and WIQ), suggesting that the former can easily act as a substitute for the latter. For comprehension of the construct, graphic scales (as opposed to questionnaires) demand very little linguistic competence by the respondent. Hence, they might be more useful in cross-cultural and comparative research on involvement-alienation. They can also be more effective when administered to less-educated samples or when time considerations do not allow the administration of longer questionnaires.

In contrast to graphic and questionnaire formats, use of the semantic-differential format (particularly the WISD scale) seems to have questionable validity. Posttest interviews of some respondents revealed that they found it difficult to relate to the abstract seven-point scales using words such as fundamental-trivial and essential-nonessential. The task of evaluating their present jobs in terms of these scales was relatively less difficult than evaluating the generalized notion of work. Because of the abstract nature of the semantic-differential format, it should be used with caution even when measuring involvement in the present job context. Perhaps its usage should be limited to only highly educated samples and in very specific contexts. For example, Edwards and Waters (1980) have used semantic-differential formats successfully with college students to measure their "academic job involvement."

These new scales for measuring job and work involvement can be used in future research to achieve several objectives. First, studies that aim at exploring the nature of job and work involvement within organizations and identifying the antecedent and consequent conditions can use these instruments. Second, the instruments can be used in studies that attempt to relate alienation and involvement in different spheres of life, such as work, family, and community. Third, tests of theoretical predictions derived from the motivational formulations on alienation and involvement can be conducted more effectively with the use of these scales. Last, the use of these scales can establish more meaningfully the cross-cultural validity and generalizability of findings related to job and work involvement.

8

MOTIVATION AND ALIENATION: SOME TESTS OF THE MOTIVATIONAL APPROACH

Let him not settle for a purely Platonic relationship with
what he already knows, in an elegant but possibly sterile
system, but see to it, rather, that in the fullness of time
the union is blessed.

Abraham Kaplan, 1964

INTRODUCTION

The usefulness of a theoretical formulation depends on the degree to which it can stand the tests of empirical validation. The motivational approach to involvement and alienation as a theoretical
formulation is no exception to this rule. It is important to establish
the scientific validity of the motivational approach by testing predictions derived from the theory. This chapter describes three different
studies that tested several such predictions.

The basic argument of the motivational approach is to maintain
a conceptual distinction between job involvement (or alienation) as a
cognitive belief state of psychological identification (or separation)
and intrinsic motivation. According to the approach, satisfaction of
intrinsic needs on the job may be a sufficient condition for job involvement, but it is not a necessary condition. While the satisfaction
of intrinsic needs on the job might increase the likelihood of increased
job involvement (or the frustration of intrinsic needs might lead to
increased job alienation) under certain conditions, it may not affect
job involvement (or alienation) under other conditions. States of job
involvement (or alienation) are more a function of satisfaction (or
frustration) of salient needs on the job, be they intrinsic or extrinsic.
Thus, according to the motivational approach, individuals with salient
extrinsic needs will be as strongly involved in their jobs as individuals

with salient intrinsic needs, provided they perceive their job to have potential for satisfying their salient needs. The above proposition is a direct contradiction to several psychological and sociological formulations discussed in Chapters 3 and 4. The three studies described in this chapter provide some empirical tests of the validity of this proposition.

The motivational approach further advocates that a clear conceptual distinction should be made between job involvement (or alienation) and work involvement (or alienation). While there are some occasional references to such a distinction in earlier literature on involvement and alienation (Blood 1969), the distinction has never been clearly thought out. The consequences of the distinction also have never been carefully examined. In the past, the common practice among researchers has been to ignore the distinction by using the terms job involvement and work involvement interchangeably. The motivational approach emphasizes the importance of such a distinction by suggesting that involvement-alienation in the contexts of a specific job and work in general represent two distinct cognitive belief states. The two belief states differ not only in terms of the objects of the belief (particular job versus work in general) but also in terms of the operational levels of the belief (descriptive versus normative belief). The two beliefs conceived this way have different etiologies. Involvement-alienation in the context of work in general (representing the moral value of work in one's life) is more a product of early socialization training, whereas involvement-alienation in the context of a specific job is more a function of the perceived need-satisfying potential of the job. On the basis of such differential etiology, the motivational approach would predict a stronger relationship of job satisfaction to job involvement than to work involvement. This prediction was tested in the studies described below.

Finally, the studies tested the prediction that job involvement is more a function of the perceived potential of the job to satisfy one's salient, rather than nonsalient, needs. The motivational approach assumes that in the job context workers consider some needs to be more important than others. Although workers look for satisfaction of all their needs, it is satisfaction of the more important needs that plays a crucial role in determining the degree of job involvement. The motivational approach, therefore, predicts that the relationship of job involvement should be stronger to more important or salient-need satisfaction than to less important or nonsalient-need satisfaction.

STUDY I

Study I* was designed to answer two major questions. First, the study examined whether there are differences between individuals whose most salient needs are intrinsic (intrinsically oriented individuals) and individuals whose most salient needs are extrinsic (extrinsically oriented individuals) with respect to their job and work involvement. In terms of the motivational approach, it was hypothesized that extrinsically oriented individuals will show as much job involvement as intrinsically oriented individuals, provided the former group of individuals experience the same level of need satisfaction in their jobs as the latter group. With a higher level of job satisfaction, the extrinsically oriented group will show greater job involvement than the intrinsically oriented group. With respect to work involvement, two groups coming from very similar sociocultural backgrounds with similar early socialization experiences will not differ from one another.

The second major question examined in the study was whether satisfaction of salient and nonsalient needs in the two groups of intrinsically and extrinsically oriented individuals leads to more or less job and work involvement. Specifically, two related hypotheses based on the motivational approach were formulated. First, it was hypothesized that for both groups of individuals with salient intrinsic and extrinsic needs the correlation between the satisfaction of salient needs and job involvement should be higher than the correlation between the satisfaction of nonsalient needs and job involvement. Second, it was also expected that for both groups the level of satisfaction of salient needs would be highly correlated with the degree of actual job involvement. No specific hypothesis, however, can be formulated with respect to the relationship between the level of salient-need satisfaction and work involvement. As mentioned earlier, involvement in the concept of work is considered to reflect a more stable normative belief not necessarily dependent on a particular job's ability to satisfy salient needs.

Method

The Job Opinion Questionnaire

This study utilized a four-part questionnaire pretested and developed earlier (Kanungo, Gorn, and Dauderis 1976; Kanungo, Misra,

---

*This study was previously reported by Gorn and Kanungo (1980).
© Copyright (1980) by Academic Press. Portions of the previous report are reprinted by permission.

and Dayal 1975). The first part was designed to provide such personal and demographic data as sex, age, level of education, income, and years of experience both within the organization and in the present job. In the second part, the respondents were required to rank 15 job factors according to their perceived importance. The 15 factors represented both intrinsic and extrinsic rewards. Based on previous research utilizing the questionnaire (Kanungo, Gorn, and Dauderis 1976), the following classification of items was employed. Eight of the factors were considered extrinsic, but organizationally controlled, job factors: adequate salary (for maintaining a good standard of living), fair pay (providing a sense of equity), promotion opportunity (to get a higher-status job), fringe benefits, job security, sound company policies, comfortable working conditions, and restricted hours or work. In addition, there were four interpersonally mediated extrinsic job outcomes: technically competent supervision, considerate supervision, good peer-group relations, and recognition (given by others for good work). The remaining three job factors were intrinsic in nature: responsibility and independence (sense of autonomy), a sense of achievement, and interesting nature of work.

In the third part of the questionnaire, the respondents were asked to indicate on a seven-point scale their present level of satisfaction or dissatisfaction in their job with respect to each of the 15 job factors. The job factors were again listed in this part of the questionnaire in random order. Besides the 15 job factors, the respondents were also asked to indicate their overall job satisfaction on a similar seven-point scale. Ordinal weights were assigned to the seven points on the scale ranging from extremely satisfied (7) to extremely dissatisfied (1). The construct and predictive validity of the particular measures used to obtain importance and satisfaction ratings from employees have been established in earlier studies (Jain, Normand, and Kanungo 1979; Kanungo, Gorn, and Dauderis 1976; Kanungo, Misra, and Dayal 1975). Part 2 (perceived importance ranking) and Part 3 (job-satisfaction scale) of the questionnaire are very similar to the ones described in the previous chapter and presented in Appendix B.

The fourth section of the questionnaire consisted of six items. The items were selected to measure job and work involvement and came from the questionnaire developed by Lodahl and Kejner (1965). The six items were divided into two categories. Three of these items were hypothesized to relate to a worker's involvement in a present job ("I usually show up for work a little early to get things ready," "I'll stay overtime to finish a job even if I'm not paid for it," and "For me, mornings at work really fly by!"). Three other items were hypothesized to relate to a worker's involvement with work in general ("You can measure a person pretty well by how good a job he does," "To me work is only a small part of who I am," and "Most things in life are more important than work"). Respondents were given a four-point, agree–disagree scale for each item. The items were scored in a manner such that higher scores reflected higher involvement.

Sample

The questionnaire described above was administered to 919 lower- to middle-level managers belonging to three job categories (administrative, sales, and technical services) in three large organizations. The cooperation of these organizations was secured. The managers were asked by their respective head offices to fill out an anonymous questionnaire that they received by mail. The managers were also requested to return the completed questionnaires by mail to the researcher's address. They were encouraged by their branch managers to participate in the study. The questionnaire return rate was 81 percent, with a range of from 75 percent to 85 percent for the three organizations. Initial analyses of the results suggested no differences in satisfaction and importance ratings among respondents in either of the three job categories or organizations. Subsequent analyses were, therefore, carried out on the total sample.

In order to select a group of managers with salient extrinsic needs (who consider the extrinsic characteristics of their job as most important) and a group of managers with salient intrinsic needs (who consider the intrinsic characteristics of their job as most important), the following procedure was used by analyzing the second part (perceived importance of job factors) of the questionnaire. For each of the 15 job factors, the percentage of managers who ranked it as most important and second most important was determined. Then the two extrinsic and two intrinsic factors that had the highest percentage figures and, therefore, were considered as most important in the overall sample were determined. These were the extrinsic factors of adequate salary and security and the intrinsic factors of interesting work and responsibility and independence. Next, the extrinsically motivated and intrinsically motivated managers were selected in the following manner. Only those managers who ranked both extrinsic factors as one and two in importance were selected to comprise the extrinsic group (N = 93) and only those who ranked both intrinsic factors as one and two in importance were selected to comprise the intrinsic group (N = 124). It was considered important to use as a criterion for selection more than one item for each group in order to obtain a more accurate classification of individuals into the intrinsic and extrinsic categories. Trying to incorporate in each of the intrinsic and extrinsic groups three items (where subjects ranked all three items as one, two, or three) resulted in too small a sample for a meaningful investigation.

It is important to note that the distinction between the intrinsic and extrinsic managers represented a classification based on the most salient needs, that is, those ranked one and two in importance. The classification, therefore, did not represent the opposite poles of the intrinsic-extrinsic dimension. The comparison of the two groups on the intrinsic-extrinsic dimension was a relative one. The intrinsic group was not solely motivated by intrinsic needs, but it was considered more intrinsically than extrinsically motivated. Likewise, the extrinsic group was not motivated only by extrinsic needs, but was considered more extrinsically than intrinsically motivated.

Procedure for Analysis of Data

Data analysis was performed on the 93 managers selected as extrinsic and the 124 managers selected as intrinsic. Biserial correlational analysis of the data from the first part of the questionnaire revealed that these two groups were of similar age, education, income, and tenure in the organization. The average age of both groups was around 34 years. Approximately half of the sample had college degrees, and the other half were high school graduates. More than 90 percent of the sample belonged to the middle-income category. Three-fourths of the sample had worked for the organization for more than ten years. The above demographic characteristics of the present sample resemble those typically found in the lower to middle levels of management in large corporations. The similar demographic characteristics of the intrinsically motivated and extrinsically motivated managers increased the likelihood that any difference in job satisfaction or involvement between the two groups was a function of extrinsic and intrinsic motivation, rather than a third variable.

A factor analysis was performed to differentiate job- and work-involvement items in Part IV of the questionnaire, and the resulting factor scores were used to compare the intrinsic and extrinsic groups on job and work involvement.

A comparison of the two groups with respect to job satisfaction was done by calculating mean satisfaction scores for each group on each of the items in Part III of the questionnaire.

Finally, to investigate the impact of salient-need satisfaction on the job and work involvement of both intrinsic and extrinsic managers, the following procedure was adopted. For the intrinsically motivated managers, their average satisfaction with the two items they ranked as most important to them (interesting work and responsibility and independence) was correlated with each of the two involvement factors. For the extrinsically motivated managers, their average satisfaction with the two items they ranked as most important (adequate salary and security) was correlated with each of the two factors. To obtain the relationship between nonsalient-need satisfaction and involvement, the average satisfaction rating on the two items that ranked lowest in importance was correlated with scores on the job- and work-involvement factors.

Results

Job and Work Involvement

The principal-components analysis of the six measures of involvement, followed by a varimax rotation, yielded two orthogonal factors. Eigenvalues of the two factors were 2.01 and 1.26, explaining 70 percent of the total variance. Factor loadings in Table 8.1 show that the various items classified themselves as predicted under two factors (job and work involvement) with but one exception. The projective item "You can measure a person pretty well by how good a job he does" loaded unexpectedly on the job involvement, rather than on the work involvement, factor. It was, therefore, included as a job-involvement item in all subsequent analyses. The emphasis on actual job performance with the phrase "how good a job he does" probably

TABLE 8.1

Factor Analysis of the Six Involvement Items from the Lodahl and Kejner Scale

	Factor 1 (job involvement)	Factor 2 (work involvement)
I'll stay overtime to finish a job even if I'm not paid for it	.65	-.09
For me, mornings at work really fly by	.82	.19
I usually show up for work a little early to get things ready	.56	.11
You can measure a person pretty well by how good a job he does	.73	.01
To me, work is a small part of who I am	.06	.95
Most things in life are more important than work	.05	.63

was linked very closely in the respondent's mind to the degree of actual job participation, rather than to the more general notion of work involvement. Perhaps the respondents associated the phrase related to good job performance with the job-participation items related to "arriving early" or "staying late," which might lead to good job performance. The internal reliability estimates for the job- and work-involvement items were .79 and .75, respectively.

Using factor scores for comparisons, the extrinsic managers for whom salary and security ranked uppermost in importance indicated more job involvement than the intrinsic managers for whom interesting work and responsibility and independence ranked uppermost in importance. The extrinsic group mean factor score was .23 (mean raw score = 2.62), and the intrinsic group mean factor score was .17 (mean raw score = 2.28). The difference between the two groups was statistically significant ($t = 3.22$, $df = 215$, $p < .01$). Although the two groups of managers differed in their job-involvement factor scores (Factor 1), there was no significant difference between their work-involvement factor scores. For Factor 2, the extrinsic group mean factor score was .06 (mean raw score = 2.62), and the intrinsic group mean factor score was .05 (mean raw score = 2.71). The t value for this comparison was 1.5, while $df = 215$, and $p > .05$.

Job Satisfaction

The motivational formulation suggests that higher job involvement is a function of higher perceived potential of the job to satisfy an individual's needs. Therefore, one might argue that the higher job-involvement scores of the extrinsic group compared with the intrinsic group should result from higher levels of job satisfaction in the extrinsic group. This possibility was tested by analyzing the job-satisfaction scores of the two groups.

The internal-reliability estimate for the 15-item job-satisfaction scale was .91. Comparing extrinsic and intrinsic managers, the extrinsic managers not only expressed greater overall satisfaction but also were more satisfied with each of the 15 job factors than the intrinsic managers. The overall multivariate F (Hotelling's T^2) was significant ($F[16,200] = 2.20$, $p < .01$). In addition, as indicated in Table 8.2, each of the individual F-tests revealed that the extrinsic group showed a significantly greater amount of satisfaction on all job-satisfaction items. Thus, the results suggest that extrinsic managers are both more satisfied and more involved in their present jobs than intrinsic managers.

TABLE 8.2

Mean Satisfaction Scores for Intrinsically and Extrinsically Motivated
Managers

Job Outcome	Intrinsic	Extrinsic	Significance Level*
Amount of security I have on my job	3.20	3.92	$p < .01$
Kind of company policies and practices that govern my job	3.04	3.78	$p < .001$
Amount of salary that I get for my job	2.91	3.36	$p < .05$
Kind of fringe benefit plans (vacation, retirement, medical, and so on) that go with my job	3.12	3.91	$p < .01$
Chances of future promotion that I have in my job	2.89	3.46	$p < .01$
Kind of working conditions (lighting, noise, office space, and so on) surrounding my job	2.93	3.80	$p < .001$
Interesting or enjoyable nature of the work in my job	2.83	3.79	$p < .001$
Amount of recognition and respect that I get for my work	2.70	3.75	$p < .001$
Opportunity I have in my job to work with people I like	2.98	3.83	$p < .001$
Technical competence of my immediate superior	2.84	3.70	$p < .001$
Opportunity that I have in my job to achieve excellence in my work	2.82	3.78	$p < .001$
Considerate and sympathetic nature of my immediate superior	3.04	3.82	$p < .01$
Kind of responsibility and independence that I have in my job	2.69	3.91	$p < .001$
Restriction of my work to office hours and the noninterference with my private life	3.29	3.86	$p < .05$
The amount of pay I get for the work I do	2.89	3.30	$p < .05$
Overall consideration, with respect to my job	2.87	3.74	$p < .001$

*Variance explained for these items, as determined by ω^2, ranged from 3 percent to 10 percent.

Relationship between Involvement and
Satisfaction of Salient versus Nonsalient Needs

It was expected that the satisfaction of salient needs would be more highly correlated with job involvement than the satisfaction of nonsalient needs in both intrinsic and extrinsic groups. Table 8.3 contains the correlations for the intrinsic and extrinsic groups between both the level of salient and nonsalient-need satisfaction and each of the two involvement factors. As indicated in Table 8.3, the correlations with the job-involvement scores were significantly higher for the satisfaction of salient needs than nonsalient needs (intrinsic group: $r = .82$ versus $r = .29$, $z = 4.00$, $p < .01$; extrinsic groups: $r = .71$ versus $r = .37$, $z = 2.29$, $p < .05$).

The correlations between the job-involvement factors and non-salient-need satisfaction were, nevertheless, significant, probably because salient need satisfaction may have a carry-over effect on nonsalient-need satisfaction. If managers are satisfied with the job outcomes they consider most important, they may tend to feel quite

TABLE 8.3

Correlations between Involvement and Salient and Nonsalient Needs
for Intrinsically and Extrinsically Motivated Managers

	Salient-Need Satisfaction	Nonsalient-Need Satisfaction
Intrinsic group		
Factor 1		
(job involvement)	.82[a]	.29[b]
Factor 2		
(work involvement)	.04	-.07
Extrinsic group		
Factor 1		
(job involvement)	.71[a]	.37[a]
Factor 2		
(work involvement)	.29[b]	.21[c]

[a] $p < .001$.
[b] $p < .01$.
[c] $p < .05$.

satisfied with their overall job and perhaps with all of the job outcomes of lesser importance as a consequence of this general overall job satisfaction. No such prediction was made with respect to the more generalized and normative belief of work involvement, since salient-need satisfaction with respect to the respondent's present job would be minimally related to involvement with the concept of work in general. In fact, the correlations between work involvement and the satisfaction of salient needs were very similar to those obtained for nonsalient needs (.04 versus .07, respectively, for the intrinsic group and .29 and .21, respectively, for the extrinsic group).

Salient-Need Satisfaction and Job Involvement

With respect to involvement in a particular job, the results in Table 8.3 suggest positive relationships between a manager's satisfaction of salient needs and involvement in the present job. This was true for both groups of managers. Thus, the degree of satisfaction with salient needs, intrinsic or extrinsic, was associated with greater involvement in the job itself.

To investigate these relationships more fully, additional analyses were performed on both the intrinsic and extrinsic managers who indicated a high degree of either satisfaction or dissatisfaction regarding the degree to which their salient needs were being met. Managers were grouped under the category "satisfied" if they ticked off one of the three points on the satisfied part of the scale for both needs they considered most important. Such a grouping yielded 45 extrinsic managers who indicated satisfaction with respect to both of their salient extrinsic needs, and 38 intrinsic managers indicating satisfaction with respect to both of their salient intrinsic needs. The same procedure was used to select "dissatisfied" managers, incorporating only those who ticked off one of the dissatisfaction points for both of their salient needs. There were 31 such extrinsic managers and 81 intrinsic managers.

Subsequently, comparisons of the job-involvement factor scores were made between satisfied and dissatisfied intrinsic managers and between satisfied and dissatisfied extrinsic managers. Such comparisons are presented in Table 8.4. As might be expected, for both the intrinsic and extrinsic groups, satisfied managers were more job involved than dissatisfied managers (rows a and c of Table 8.4). Directly comparing the intrinsic group with the extrinsic group, the data revealed a similarity between the two groups (row e of Table 8.4). Thus, not only was the level of satisfaction correlated with job involvement for both the intrinsic and extrinsic groups, but their absolute level of job involvement when the level of satisfaction was controlled was also the same; satisfied and dissatisfied extrinsic

TABLE 8.4

Job- and Work-Involvement Factor Scores for Satisfied and
Dissatisfied Intrinsically and Extrinsically Motivated Managers

	Satisfied	Dissatisfied	t-value	ω^2
Intrinsic				
a. Factor 1				
(job involvement)	.90(3.12)	-.74(1.83)	16.63[a]	.70
b. Factor 2				
(work involvement)	.09(2.75)	.02(2.72)	.34	.00
Extrinsic				
c. Factor 1				
(job involvement)	.74(3.02)	-.62(1.95)	11.32[a]	.63
d. Factor 2				
(work involvement)	.16(2.82)	-.47(2.23)	2.99[a]	.10
Intrinsic versus extrinsic				
t-values				
e. Factor 1				
(job involvement)				
t	-1.37	1.16		
ω^2	.01	.00		
f. Factor 2				
(work involvement)				
t	.37	2.12[b]		
ω^2	.00	.03		

[a] $p < .001$.
[b] $p < .05$.

Note: Raw score means for the items in each factor are contained in parentheses.

managers showed the same level of job involvement as their intrinsic
counterparts.

Salient-Need Satisfaction and Work Involvement

With respect to work involvement, the correlation between the
level of need satisfaction and the work-involvement factor scores was

significant only for the extrinsic group (see Table 8.3). The near-
zero correlation for the intrinsic group stems from the fact that both
satisfied and dissatisfied intrinsically motivated managers attached
a moderate level of importance to work in their life, with an average
mean score of 2.75 and 2.72 on the two measures of work involvement (see row b of Table 8.4). As might be expected with a similarity
of two means, the work-involvement factor scores for the satisfied
and dissatisfied intrinsic managers were not significantly different.
However, there was a clearer differentiation of responses between
satisfied and dissatisfied extrinsically motivated managers in their
average responses to the two measures of work involvement (see row
d of Table 8.4). Looking at the scores in Table 8.4, it seems that it
was only the satisfied managers in the extrinsic group that valued
work in general in a way similar to the intrinsic group. Thus, only
one (extrinsically oriented and job-dissatisfied) of the four groups of
managers showed lower work involvement. Whether a culturally conditioned belief regarding the value of work is affected by job dissatisfaction among extrinsically oriented individuals is an issue that requires further verification.

Conclusion

The results from this study support the proposed distinction between two kinds of involvement: involvement in a particular job and
involvement with work in general. Using the items from the Lodahl
and Kejner (1965) scales, the study also demonstrates how the two
kinds of involvement have been confused in earlier research. Factor
analysis of the six items selected for the study clearly revealed the
two factors of job and work involvement. Furthermore, the construct
validity of these factors is revealed by the predicted relationship between the level of salient-need satisfaction and the degree of actual
job involvement that was expected and obtained for both intrinsic and
extrinsic managers. In addition, as mentioned in the methods section, the procedures utilized in this study focused on distinguishing
between groups of managers who were relatively more intrinsically
or extrinsically motivated, rather than between groups who were at
the extreme poles on the intrinsic-extrinsic motivation dimension.
It is possible that if future research discovers a greater separation
between the intrinsic and extrinsic groups, then the findings obtained
in the present study might come out even stronger.

One interesting finding in the present study was that extrinsic
managers were on the whole more satisfied and more involved with
their particular jobs. This result is consistent with the findings of
a recent comparative study (Kanungo 1980). This study found that

Francophone managers who were relatively more extrinsically motivated than Anglophone managers also showed a greater degree of job satisfaction and involvement. The fact that extrinsic managers showed less job dissatisfaction than intrinsic managers (see Table 8.2) was further supported by another finding in the present study. In selecting the dissatisfied managers for analysis, we were able to find only 31 out of 93 individuals (33 percent) in the extrinsic group who felt dissatisfied with both of their very important extrinsic needs, whereas 81 out of 124 such dissatisfied people (65 percent) existed in the intrinsic group. Managers with high intrinsic needs would seem not easily satisfied, perhaps because of their high expectations about the nature of a job they should have and/or the relative difficulty management may have in structuring a job that can in fact be interesting and offer self-development, independence, and so on. It is difficult to provide jobs that one could describe as truly intrinsically rewarding, but it is perhaps relatively easy to offer jobs with good pay and security.

If the profile of a relatively more easily satisfied and job-involved manager who is motivated primarily by extrinsic factors holds true, then the findings have important implications for organizational decisions. For example, as far as involvement in a particular job is concerned, the results of this study suggest that organizations may have little to gain but a great deal to lose by either favoring intrinsically motivated individuals in their hiring and promotional practices or by instituting programs within the organization to stimulate intrinsic motivation (for example, quality of working life or achievement training sessions).

While the extrinsic managers indicated more job satisfaction and job involvement than the intrinsic managers, the results of the present study also supported the hypothesis that satisfaction of the extrinsic or hygiene job factors (Herzberg 1966) for extrinsically motivated people and satisfaction of intrinsic factors or motivators for intrinsically motivated people were equally likely to create high job involvement. When the level of satisfaction was controlled, equal levels of satisfaction or dissatisfaction produced equal levels of job involvement in the intrinsic and extrinsic groups (Table 8.4). Similar results supporting the above hypothesis were reported recently by Misra and Kalro (1981). Their findings, based on a sample of managers in India, suggest cross-cultural generalizability of the hypothesis. Results of studies based on the motivational approach, therefore, provide little evidence to support the notion that the satisfaction of intrinsic needs represents the satisfaction of a higher plane of needs in that it is more closely linked to greater job involvement.

When it comes to involvement with work in general, dissatisfied extrinsic managers tended to attach lesser importance to work than satisfied extrinsic and intrinsic managers and dissatisfied intrinsic managers. One could speculate that job satisfaction plays a role in encouraging extrinsic managers to value work, whereas satisfaction may be less important in determining the work involvement of intrinsic managers. Since the importance attached to work in general reflects a cognitive predisposition that an individual presumably carries from one situation to another, perhaps the intrinsically motivated person might still consider work as a central aspect of a self-image, even if one is dissatisfied with a particular job. Such a hypothesis would suggest no difference in work involvement between satisfied and dissatisfied managers in the intrinsic group, which was in fact the case. Further research conducted in different organizational settings and with different operational definitions and measures of both involvement (job or work) and motivation (intrinsic and extrinsic) are needed to test the hypothesis.

STUDY II

Study II utilized the data obtained for the development of new job- and work-involvement scales described in Chapter 7. The purpose of this study was to test several theoretical predictions derived from the motivational approach and thereby establish the predictive validity of the theory and the concurrent validity of the new measures of job and work involvement.

It may be recalled that a questionnaire was administered to a heterogeneous sample of 703 respondents. The data gathered from these respondents contained information on five things: demographic characteristics, such as income, age, and education; the perceived importance of 15 job outcomes, which included both intrinsic and extrinsic outcomes; experienced level of satisfaction with these outcomes, as measured by a 15-item satisfaction scale and overall job satisfaction measured by a single item; degree of job involvement as measured by three different scales (JISD, JIQ, and JIG); and degree of work involvement as measured by three different scales (WISD, WIQ, and WIG). Information on the respondents' demographic characteristics, their perceived importance of job outcomes, and the level of their job satisfaction were used to test the criterion-related concurrent validity of the job- and work-involvement scales. Based on the motivational approach, the following hypotheses were formulated and tested in the study. It may be noticed that the first three hypotheses are very similar to the ones described and tested in Study I.

Hypotheses

Hypothesis 1: Measures of job involvement compared with measures of work involvement should be more strongly associated with measures of job satisfaction.

This hypothesis is based on the fact that job involvement stems primarily from the perception of a need-satisfying potential for the job (contemporaneous causation), while work involvement is more a matter of past socialization and cultural conditioning (historical causation).

Hypothesis 2: Measures of job involvement will be more strongly associated with the satisfaction of salient (most important) rather than nonsalient (least important) needs on the job. This pattern of relationships is not expected in the case of work-involvement measures.

This hypothesis is based on the assumption that the satisfaction of salient needs on the job is more crucial in increasing job involvement than the satisfaction of nonsalient needs. However, satisfaction of either salient or nonsalient needs does not directly influence work involvement. Work involvement is a historically and culturally conditioned normative belief and is not dependent on satisfaction with the present job outcomes.

Hypothesis 3: Individuals with salient extrinsic needs are as likely to be involved in their jobs as individuals with salient intrinsic needs, provided they experience equal levels of satisfaction with present job outcomes.

According to the motivational approach, the state of job involvement refers to a cognitive belief of psychological identification with the job. Such a state must be distinguished from intrinsic motivation (or on-the-job satisfaction of salient intrinsic needs). As a cognitive belief state, job involvement results from the perceived potential of the job to satisfy one's salient needs. Thus, in intrinsically motivated individuals job involvement can result from satisfaction of their salient intrinsic needs, and in extrinsically motivated individuals it can result from satisfaction of their salient extrinsic needs.

Hypothesis 4: The measure of job and work involvement will have different patterns of relationship to demographic variables, such as income, age, and seniority.

Job and work involvement are distinct concepts. The former is a more specific and descriptive belief about the present job, while the latter is a more general and normative belief about work in general. As a specific descriptive belief, the job involvement of individuals is influenced by their perceived job outcomes. Significant variations in individuals' perceptions of job outcomes, therefore, should be related to variations in job involvement. Changes in salary level, seniority, and job level (through promotion, demotion, or transfer) may result in significant variations in perceived job outcomes and consequent job involvement in individuals. Likewise, at any given time, individuals with different demographic characteristics, such as belonging to different levels of income, seniority, or age will experience different levels of perceived job outcomes. As a result, they will also show different levels of job involvement. Thus, job involvement will be expected to correlate with demographic characteristics, such as income level, seniority, and age.

Work involvement, on the other hand, may not be related either to temporal changes in perceived job outcomes or to different levels of demographic characteristics. Work involvement is conceived as a culturally conditioned, normative belief about work in general. Such a normative belief is likely to be more stable and more resistant to the influence of environmental changes (causing variations in perceived job outcomes) from time to time. Individuals are more likely to carry such normative beliefs from one situation to another. Since work involvement is more a function of prior socialization and cultural background, it will not vary with different levels of demographic characteristics of respondents, as long as the respondents share similar cultural and socialization experience.

Hypothesis 5: Individuals with a higher income will show higher job satisfaction and consequently higher job involvement. No such relationship is expected for work involvement.

This is a more specific hypothesis; the reasons for this are described under Hypothesis 4. Since money can satisfy a number of intrinsic and extrinsic needs of individuals (Lawler 1971), those who get paid more in their job are likely to see a greater potential for their job to satisfy their needs. A job that has a greater need-satisfying potential is also more involving.

Results

In order to examine the relationship of job satisfaction to job and work involvement, the six involvement scales were correlated with the two measures of job satisfaction: the 15-item job-satisfaction scale and the single-item overall-satisfaction index. The reliability coefficient of these two measures for the present sample is

TABLE 8.5

Correlation of Involvement Scales with Job-Satisfaction Measures

Scale	Job-Satisfaction Scale	Overall Job-Satisfaction Index
JISD	-.27*	-.56*
WISD	-.01	-.08
t	5.96*	12.79*
JIQ	.57*	.43*
WIQ	.12*	.04
t	12.18*	9.64*
JIG	.65*	.55*
WIG	.24*	.06
t	12.61*	13.94*

*p < .01.

presented in Chapter 7 (see Table 7.3). Besides, as parallel-form tests of job satisfaction, the two measures correlate substantially (r = .78). The correlations of the six involvement scales with each of the two satisfaction measures are presented in Table 8.5. The results in Table 8.5 clearly support the first hypothesis that job-satisfaction measures have a stronger relationship to job-involvement measures than to work-involvement measures.

The second hypothesis that job involvement is more a function of salient-need satisfaction was tested in the following manner. The perceived importance rankings of the 15 job factors were analyzed to determine the saliency of the needs of the respondents. For every respondent, salient need was defined as the two job outcomes that were ranked by the respondent as first and second in order of importance. The nonsalient need was defined as the two job outcomes that were ranked by the respondent as fourteenth and fifteenth in importance. The respondent's satisfaction scores on the two salient job outcomes were added to represent a single score for salient-need satisfaction. Likewise, the respondent's satisfaction scores on the two nonsalient job outcomes were added to represent a single score for nonsalient-need satisfaction. Each of the six involvement-scale scores was then correlated with the salient and nonsalient need-satisfaction scores. The results are presented in Table 8.6. As

TABLE 8.6

Correlation of Involvement Scores with Salient- and Nonsalient-Need
Satisfaction

Scale	Salient-Need Satisfaction	Nonsalient-Need Satisfaction	t
JISD	-.24*	-.12*	3.06*
JIQ	.49*	.31*	5.47*
JIG	.56*	.32*	7.21*
WISD	-.02	-.07	.05
WIQ	.10*	.10*	.00
WIG	.18*	.16*	0.51

*p < .01.

expected, the job-involvement measures correlated more strongly
with salient- than nonsalient-need satisfaction. This pattern, however, was not observed for the work-involvement measures.

The third prediction regarding the job involvement of intrinsic-
and extrinsic-oriented respondents was tested by following the procedure described earlier in Study I. A group of intrinsic (N = 76) and
a group of extrinsic (N = 42) respondents were chosen on the basis of
their perceived importance of job-outcome rankings. Each member
of the intrinsic group perceived the two intrinsic outcomes, interesting nature of work and responsibility, as being the two most important
job outcomes. Each member of the extrinsic group, on the other hand,
perceived the two extrinsic outcomes, money and security, as the two
most important job outcomes. The choice of these outcomes to represent intrinsic and extrinsic needs depended on two criteria. These
outcomes are clearly distinguishable as intrinsic and extrinsic outcomes, and, within the intrinsic and extrinsic categories, these outcomes were cited most frequently in the overall sample as the first
or second-ranking job outcome.

The mean scores of the six involvement scales for the two groups
are presented in Table 8.7. Controlling for the level of job satisfaction, the involvement scores of the two groups were compared through
covariance analyses. Separate analysis of covariance was performed
for each of the six involvement-scale scores, treating job-satisfaction
scores (on the 15-item scale) as the covariant. The results in Table

TABLE 8.7

Involvement Scores of Intrinsic and Extrinsic Groups

| Scale | Intrinsic (N = 76) | | Extrinsic (N = 42) | | |
	Mean	Standard Deviation	Mean	Standard Deviation	$F(1/115)$
JISD	20.88	8.99	23.81	8.44	3.45
JIQ	33.41	10.26	32.41	8.24	0.36
JIG	9.10	2.53	8.31	2.83	3.76
WISD	19.78	7.95	18.93	7.71	0.57
WIQ	21.06	4.80	20.83	6.32	0.51
WIG	9.43	1.68	9.00	2.77	1.11

8.7 reveal insignificant F-values (df = 1/115, p > .05) in each case. This confirms the expectation that, with equal levels of job satisfaction, job involvement of intrinsic and extrinsic individuals will not differ.

The two groups also did not differ with respect to their work involvement. It is quite conceivable that two groups of respondents may view work in general to be of equal importance in their lives because of a common cultural emphasis on the centrality of work. It is also possible that the two groups may attach equal importance to work in their lives for different motivational reasons. Intrinsically motivated individuals may have learned through past socialization to value work because it can satisfy their intrinsic needs for autonomy, responsibility, and so on. Extrinsically motivated individuals may have also learned in the past to consider work as central to one's life because work can provide them with extrinsic-need satisfaction.

In order to test Hypotheses 4 and 5, the patterns of relationship of job- and work-involvement measures to demographic variables were examined. Previous studies in the area of job and work involvement (Aldag and Brief 1975; Cherrington, Condie, and England 1979; Rabinowitz and Hall 1977; Saal 1981) have reported a statistically significant relationship of five demographic variables to job involvement. These variables are age, education, income, seniority or tenure in an organization, and sex. Correlations of these variables with each of the six involvement measures are presented in Table 8.8. None of the demographic variables had any significant relationship

TABLE 8.8

Correlation between Demographic Variables and Involvement
Measures

	Demographic Variables				
	Age	Education	Income	Security	Sex
Job-involvement scales					
JISD	-.18*	-.02	-.24*	-.17*	.02
JIQ	.19*	.01	.24*	.18*	.00
JIG	.24*	.00	.27*	.18*	.02
Work-involvement scales					
WISD	-.02	-.06	-.04	-.01	.07
WIQ	.05	.02	.02	.00	-.02
WIG	.01	.00	.08	.02	.00

*$p < .01$.

Note: In the case of JISD and WISD scales, lower scores represent higher involvement.

to work-involvement measures. However, three demographic variables (age, seniority, and income) have significant relationships to each of the job-involvement measures. With increasing age, seniority, and income level, job involvement tended to increase. No such relationship was evident for work involvement. These results support Hypothesis 4, which says that job and work involvement have different patterns of relationship to the demographic variables.

Two additional issues need some further discussion at this point. First, the results in Table 8.8 reveal that the educational levels and sex of the respondents are not significantly related to job-involvement measures. Although some earlier studies have noticed significant relationships of sex and educational levels to job involvement, such results cannot be considered reliable because of methodological problems associated with job-involvement measures used in these studies. For instance, Saal (1981) reported a significant relationship between sex and job involvement ($r = -.19$) and between education and job involvement ($r = .14$) when job involvement was measured by Lodahl and Kejner's (1965) item scale. But no such relationship was obtained

TABLE 8.9

Intercorrelations among Five Demographic Variables

	Age	Education	Income	Seniority	Sex
Age	—	.08	.46*	.53*	.00
Education		—	.22*	-.05	-.18
Income			—	.32*	-.21*
Seniority				—	-.04
Sex					—

*$p < .01$.

TABLE 8.10

Multiple Regression Analysis of the Correlates of Job-Involvement
Measures

Variables Entered	R	Change in R^2	B	F-Ratio
JISD scale				
Income	.236	.056	-.199	19.098*
Seniority	.252	.007	-.064	1.928
Age	.255	.002	-.054	1.225
Education	.257	.001	.024	0.358
Sex	.257	.000	-.014	0.132
JIQ scale				
Income	.239	.057	.207	20.949*
Seniority	.260	.010	.073	2.523
Education	.266	.003	-.055	1.865
Age	.271	.003	.059	1.510
Sex	.273	.001	.035	0.782
JIG scale				
Income	.267	.071	.216	23.014*
Age	.295	.016	.120	6.158*
Education	.299	.002	-.042	1.137
Seniority	.301	.001	.035	0.583
Sex	.301	.000	.023	0.332

*$p < .01$.

by Saal (1981) when job involvement was measured by a three-item
scale. The three-item scale measured job involvement as a cognitive
state of psychological identification and, therefore, was similar to the
scales used in the present study. It seems that job involvement viewed
as a cognitive belief state (as defined in the motivational approach) is
not significantly related to either sex or education of the respondents
(at least in U.S. and Canadian samples).

The second issue concerns the problem of intercorrelations
among the demographic variables themselves. The intercorrelations
among these variables are presented in Table 8.9. It may be noticed
in Table 8.9 that age, seniority, and income tend to be positively related to each other. Although the results in Table 8.8 suggest that
an increase in each of the three variables is associated with an increase in job involvement, it is not clear which of the variables explain how much variance in job involvement, since all three of them
covary together. Besides, in order to test Hypothesis 5, it is necessary to assess how income level alone is related to job involvement.
For the assessment of the relative contributions of each of the demographic variables to job involvement, stepwise multiple-regression
analyses were performed on the data. Three different analyses, one
for each dependent job-involvement measure, were performed. In
each case, the five demographic variables served as the independent
variables. The results are presented in Table 8.10. Inspection of
Table 8.10 suggests that when all five demographic variables were
allowed to compete freely to enter into a stepwise regression, income
or salary level always entered as the first variable and explained 6
percent to 7 percent of the variance in job involvement. It is quite
clear from the beta values in the case of all three scales that with
higher income levels, job involvement tends to increase. In the case
of the JIG scale, along with income level, age had some significant
effect.

The above analysis supports Hypothesis 5, which predicts an increase in job involvement with an increase in the income level of respondents. The reason for this positive relationship can be attributed
to the relationship between higher income level and job satisfaction.
According to the motivational approach, any variable that would increase the perceived potential of the job to satisfy one's needs would
also increase job involvement. Since salary or income level is considered a potential variable that may be related to job satisfaction, it was
predicted that an income variable would also be related to job involvement. In order to find out whether the income variable was, in fact,
related to job satisfaction, the variable was correlated with three satisfaction measures: satisfaction with one's pay, the single-item overall
job-satisfaction index, and the 15-item job satisfaction scale. The
correlations of income level with the three satisfaction measures were

.32, .20, and .29, respectively. All correlations are statistically significant at the .01 level of confidence. These results provide support for the contention that higher income from a job brings in higher job satisfaction, which in turn results in higher job involvement.

Conclusion

Taken together, Study I and Study II provide strong validation for support of the motivational approach to job and work involvement. The two studies have used two different managerial samples and different instruments to measure job and work involvement, and yet both studies have obtained similar results, which confirm a set of predictions derived from the motivational approach. This attests to the fact that the results are not method bound and that they are generalizable from one heterogeneous sample to another.

Study II provided several tests of criterion-related concurrent validity of the new measures of job and work involvement described in the previous chapter. In addition, Study II revealed some evidence on the role of extrinsic job outcomes, such as salary in job involvement. Very often, researchers have neglected the powerful motivating role of salary as a job outcome. Influenced by the humanistic tradition of the 1960s (Herzberg 1966; McGregor 1960), researchers have underplayed the role of salary and have even considered that motivating employees through an increased salary is detrimental to the development of job involvement. The results of Study II provide evidence against this humanistic-tradition-based thinking. The results clearly indicate that salary has a potential influence on both job satisfaction and involvement. It is, in fact, one of the more concrete and manipulable job outcomes that can be utilized for influencing employee satisfaction and involvement.

STUDY III

The third study was designed specifically to explore the distinctness or commonality of job involvement (as a cognitive belief of psychological identification with the job) and intrinsic motivational orientations of workers. Earlier psychological and sociological approaches have suggested a great degree of commonality between job involvement and intrinsic motivational orientation. The motivational approach, however, argues for the distinctness of the two variables. One way to investigate whether the two variables are distinct from each other or have a high degree of commonality is to assess their relationships to a criterion variable. The present study adopted this strategy.

Positive mental health was selected as the criterion variable, and its relationship to job involvement and intrinsic orientation was explored.

The Concept of Mental Health

There is considerable conceptual ambiguity with regard to the construct of mental health. As yet, there is no single, universally acceptable definition of mental health. Moreover, the definition of mental health is bound to reflect cultural values (Jahoda 1958). Behavior that is considered as an indication of mental health in one society may not be considered a sign of mental health in another. Thus, the concept is to a large extent culture specific. Given this limitation, several attempts have been made during the last two decades to define and operationalize the concept of mental health in the United States (Bradburn and Caplovitz 1965; French 1963; Kasl 1974; Kornhauser 1965; Quinn, Seashore, Kahn, Mangione, Campbell, Staines, and McCullough 1971). These attempts have viewed mental health in different ways, such as the overall level of personal success, personal satisfaction, personal effectiveness, or socially considerate behavior. Even mental health is viewed from a Marxian perspective and is considered as a disguised formulation of the Marxian concept of alienation (Seeman 1975).

In spite of such diverse views on the nature of mental health, there seems to be some general agreement on its multidimensionality. Kasl (1973), for example, suggested four different criteria on the basis of which mental health is assessed. The criteria are functional effectiveness, well-being, mastery and competence, and psychiatric signs and symptoms. Likewise, Kornhauser (1965), whose conceptualization and operationalization of mental health is widely used in empirical literature, has provided a more comprehensive framework. He identified six dimensions of mental health. These dimensions are manifest anxiety and emotional tension, feeling of self-esteem, feeling of hostility toward other people, sociability and friendship, overall satisfaction with life, and personal morale. These dimensions were derived empirically from an industrial setting. Kornhauser developed six indexes, each measuring one of the above dimensions reflecting specific aspects of mental health. Taken together the six indexes comprise the operational definition of mental health. Kornhauser's original measures of mental health were based on structured interviews and required time-consuming coding procedures. Recently, however, for the sake of research convenience several researchers have developed and used paper-and-pencil questionnaire tests to measure the six dimensions and the composite index of mental health as conceived by Kornhauser (Gechman and Wiener 1975; Jamal and Mitchell 1980).

In the present study, Kornhauser's formulation of mental health was chosen to represent the criterion variable because of its comprehensiveness and methodologically sound operationalization. However, instead of using Kornhauser's interviewing and coding procedure to arrive at the indexes of mental health, the study used the questionnaire developed by Jamal, Barnowe, and Mitchell (1977). In order to provide the reader with a better grasp of Kornhauser's six dimensions of mental health, some examples of items measuring each dimension are presented below. In the questionnaire developed by Jamal, Barnowe, and Mitchell (1977), the first dimension (level of anxiety) is measured by responses on a five-point scale (registering frequency of occurrence, degree of agreement, and so on) to items such as "I am often worried and upset" and "I worry much about things that might happen to me." Likewise, the second dimension (degree of self-esteem) is measured by using items such as "I feel that I can do much to make my future what I want it to be" or "I often have a hard time to make up my mind." The third dimension (feeling of hostility) is measured by items such as "I sometimes feel like smashing things for no good reason" or "I often have to tell people to mind their own business." The fourth dimension (sociability) is measured by items such as "How often do you get together with your relatives?" or "In the last four weeks, approximately how many hours did you spend in attending the meetings of various organizations?" The fifth dimension (overall life satisfaction) is measured by items such as "I feel in good spirits almost all the time" or "I have as much chance to enjoy life as I should have." Finally, the sixth dimension (personal morale—considered as the opposite of anomie, social alienation, or despair) is measured by items such as "Nowadays a person has to live pretty much for today and let tomorrow take care of itself" or "It is hardly fair to bring children into the world with the way things look for the future."

Mental Health and Intrinsic-Extrinsic Orientation

In the job situation an intrinsically oriented person looks for job outcomes that will satisfy salient needs for personal success or achievement, independence, responsibility, and self-esteem. An extrinsically oriented person, on the other hand, will be more concerned with job outcomes such as security, social approval, working conditions, and salary that will satisfy salient extrinsic needs. How would such intrinsic-extrinsic job orientation of individuals be related to their mental health? The question can be resolved if one closely

analyzes the nature of the mental health construct and its operational
measures as proposed by Kornhauser (1965). In a validation study of
the mental health index, Kornhauser proposes the following description of what constitutes the essential characteristics of mental health:
(1) "effective, mature reactions to life conditions and to people (in the
light of person's opportunities and abilities)"; (2) "adjustment through
active, reality-oriented decisions and appropriate efforts at mastery
of environment (rather than solely through passive conformity)"; (3)
"realistic acceptance of self, self-respect; relatively stable, consistent, integrated personality (relatively free from disrupting inner
conflict)"; (4) "self-reliance, zest, acceptance of responsibilities;
planning ahead, healthy independence and emotional control"; (5)
"warm, friendly interpersonal relations"; and (6) "relative freedom
from interfering neurotic symptoms and defensive reactions" (pp.
323-24). One can easily notice in the above description of mental
health several characteristics that can be attributed to intrinsically
oriented individuals. Like the characteristics of mentally healthy individuals, intrinsic individuals also look for opportunities to utilize
their abilities effectively to achieve personal success, accept more
responsibility, plan ahead, feel independent, have control over their
environment, and so on. On the basis of such similarities between
the two constructs (mental health and intrinsic orientation), it is only
natural to expect the composite mental health index to positively correlate with intrinsic orientation.

A closer scrutiny of the items in the Jamal, Barnowe, and
Mitchell (1977) questionnaire for measuring each of the six mental
health dimensions reveals that two of the dimensions (self-esteem
and personal morale) closely resemble the characteristics of self-
assuredness, independence, and achievement orientation of intrinsic
individuals. Thus, it is expected that measures of these two dimensions should positively correlate with intrinsic orientation. No such
relationship is expected for the remaining four dimensions of mental
health.

Mental Health and Job Involvement

According to the motivational approach, job involvement refers
to a cognitive state of psychological identification with the job. How
should such a cognitive state be related to the mental health index?
There is very little empirical research that can throw light on
the issue of the relationship between job involvement and mental
health. A study by Gechman and Wiener (1975) found as statistically
insignificant the relationship (r = .10) between job involvement and
mental health. However, the results of the study cannot be considered

reliable, because job involvement was measured in the study using the Lodahl and Kejner (1965) scale. As discussed earlier in the book, the Lodahl and Kejner scale has serious construct-validity problems; the scale includes not only items that represent psychological identification with the job but also items that represent intrinsic motivation on the job.

Although empirical research evidence is lacking in the area, several anecdotal evidences (Oates 1971) suggest that job involvement may be negatively related to mental health. Several researchers (Gechman and Wiener 1975; Jahoda 1958; Korman and Korman 1980) have alluded to this possibility. Since mental health implies well-rounded participation and adjustments in other areas of life, such as the family, community, and avocational activities, excessive job involvement may interfere with participation and adjustments in other spheres of life. Furthermore, workaholic habits resulting from excessive job involvement (or complete identification with one's job) may cause physical, psychosomatic, and emotional problems both on and off the job. For these reasons, one might expect job involvement to be negatively related not only to the composite index of mental health but also to specific dimensions of mental health representing emotional problems, such as anxiety and hostility indexes.

Method

Questionnaire and the Variables Measured

The questionnaire used in the study has four parts. Part I of the questionnaire contains the ten-item JIQ scale. The psychometric properties of the JIQ scale, its reliability and validity, were discussed in Study II, as well as in the previous chapter. Part II of the questionnaire contains the 60-item Job Attitude Scale (JAS) developed by Saleh (1971). Each item in the JAS presents a pair of intrinsic and extrinsic job outcomes, and the respondent is asked to show a preference for one of them. Thus, the scale provides an intrinsic orientation score ranging from 0 to 60. Saleh (1964, 1971) has reported a split-half reliability of .94 and test-retest reliability of .88 for this scale. Other psychometric properties of the JAS are discussed in detail in a report by Saleh (1971). Part III of the questionnaire contains the measures of mental health developed by Jamal, Barnowe, and Mitchell (1977). The measures include six subscales corresponding to Kornhauser's (1965) six dimensions: anxiety, self-esteem, hostility, sociability, life satisfaction, and personal morale. These subscales are slightly modified by excluding items that measure more than one dimension. Data on the construction and validation of these subscales are reported by Jamal, Barnowe, and Mitchell (1977) and by Jamal and Mitchell (1980). In earlier studies, reliabilities of these subscales ranged from .60 to .93, with a median of .89 (Jamal and Mitchell 1980). The final part of the questionnaire is designed to obtain demographic information (such as age and sex) about the respondents.

Sample and Procedure

The sample consisted of 132 full-time employees belonging to various organizations in and around Montreal. These employees were enrolled in evening courses offered at two different universities. The questionnaire was administered to the employees at the universities during class hours. The employees were asked not to reveal their identity in any form and were assured of the confidentiality of their responses.

Results

Analysis of the demographic characteristics revealed that the sample was quite heterogeneous in its composition. Of the respondents, 39 percent were between 20 and 25 years of age; 44 percent were between 26 and 35 years of age; and 17 percent were above 35 years of age. Approximately half of them were married. Their education ranged from high school to the graduate level. Two-thirds of the sample were male, and one-third was female. Approximately half of the sample earned more than $18,000 per year. The tenure in the organization where the respondents worked ranged from one year to more than ten years, and they came from various organizational sectors (hospital, school, manufacturing, communication, transportation, labor, and government).

Relationship of Mental Health to
Job Involvement and Intrinsic Orientation

For each respondent, six mental health indexes, representing six dimensions of mental health, and a composite index were calculated. In calculating the composite index, each of the six dimensions were given equal weight. Since there was no evidence in the available literature suggesting differential weights for these dimensions, it was assumed that each dimension contributed equally to the total mental health of the respondent. All these mental health indexes were correlated with one another and with the job-involvement and intrinsic-orientation scores of the respondents. The job-involvement and intrinsic-orientation scores were also correlated with each other. The intercorrelation matrix is presented in Table 8.11. In Table

TABLE 8.11

Intercorrelations among Mental Health, Job-Involvement, and Intrinsic-Orientation Measures

Variables Measured	1	2	3	4	5	6	7	8	9
1. Freedom from anxiety	—	.41	.35	-.09	.64	.31	.67	-.23	.23
2. Self-esteem		—	.57	.04	.25	.42	.61	-.16	.25
3. Freedom from hostility			—	.25	.14	.58	.69	-.18	.31
4. Sociability				—	-.07	.11	.39	-.05	.07
5. Life satisfaction					—	.24	.70	-.10	.08
6. Personal morale						—	.64	.00	.31
7. Composite index							—	-.24	.31
8. Job involvement								—	-.05
9. Intrinsic orientation									—

Note: Correlations of .17 or more are significant at the .05 level of confidence. The correlations in the triangle represent relationships among mental health subscales. The correlations under column 7 represent relationships of subscales with the composite mental health index. The correlations in the rectangle show the relationship of mental health measures with job involvement and intrinsic orientation. The circled correlation represents the relationship between job involvement and intrinsic job orientation.

147

8.11, the correlations inside the triangle represent relationships among the mental health subscales. It should be noticed that the dimension of sociability is not significantly related to other dimensions, except for hostility. The relative independence of the sociability dimension is also reflected in its correlation with the composite index. Kornhauser (1965) also reported similar results. In his study, when the dimensions were intercorrelated, the smallest correlation coefficients involved the sociability index. According to Kornhauser, low sociability may reflect high "anxiety and inadequacy with consequent withdrawal" for some persons; for other persons, it may represent "high self-sufficiency, self-esteem, and nondependence" (p. 29). This may be the reason for the relative independence of the sociability dimension. The correlations of the subscales with the composite index are all significant. They are presented under column 7 in Table 8.11. The circled correlation (r = -.05) in Table 8.11, representing the relationship of job involvement and intrinsic job orientation, clearly suggests the independence and distinctiveness of the two variables.

Finally, the correlations included in the rectangle in Table 8.11 represent the relationship of job involvement and intrinsic orientation to seven different mental health measures. The negative significant correlations of job involvement with the composite mental health measure (r = -.24) confirms the expectation that too much job involvement may be detrimental to one's mental health. Furthermore, such a detrimental effect on mental health manifests itself more clearly in the areas of anxiety and hostility. These two dimensions of mental health show significant negative correlations ($r_s = -.23$ and $r_s = -.18$, respectively) with job involvement.

In contrast to the negative relationship of job involvement to mental health, the relationship of intrinsic job orientation to mental health was found to be positive. The intrinsic-orientation scores have a significant positive correlation (r = .31) with the composite mental health index. As expected, intrinsic orientation was also found to be significantly and positively related to two dimensions of mental health (self-esteem and personal morale). In addition, however, the intrinsic orientation was also significantly related to the freedom-from-hostility dimension. Since intrinsically oriented individuals tend to trust their own ability (because of higher self-esteem and self-assuredness), it is quite likely that they would also have trust in others. Trust in one's self and in others may reduce hostile tendencies in the individual.

The positive relation of mental health to intrinsic orientation and the negative relation of mental health to job involvement suggest that individuals with high intrinsic orientation and low job involvement should exhibit the highest level of mental health. For the same rea-

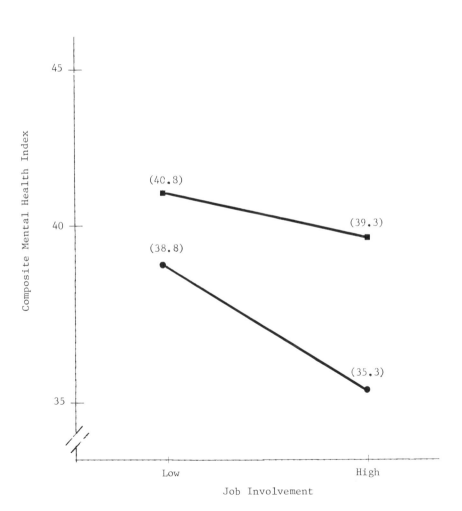

FIGURE 8.1

Mental Health Index of Intrinsic and Extrinsic Groups with High and
Low Job Involvement

FIGURE 8.2

Mental Health Index of High and Low Job Involvement and High and
Low Intrinsic (Intrinsic and Extrinsic) Categories of Respondents

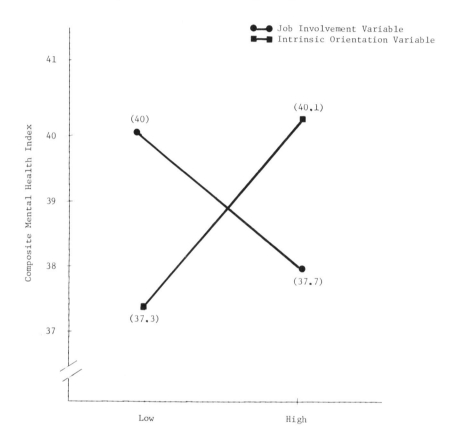

sons, individuals with low intrinsic (or high extrinsic) orientation and
high job involvement should exhibit the lowest level of mental health.
In order to verify this expectation, the respondents were classified
into four groups: intrinsic-high involvement, intrinsic-low involvement, extrinsic-high involvement, and extrinsic-low involvement.
The classification was based on intrinsic-orientation and involvement
scores. Since the possible range of intrinsic-orientation scores was
from 0 to 60, respondents with scores above 30 were classified under
the intrinsic category, and those with scores below 30 were classified
under the extrinsic category. The possible range of job involvement
scores was from 10 to 60. The respondents with scores above 35
were classified under the high-involvement category, and those with

scores below 35 were classified under the low-involvement category. Six respondents with an intrinsic score of 30 or an involvement score of 35 were eliminated from the analysis. This procedure resulted in 36 respondents in the intrinsic-high involvement group, 37 respondents in the intrinsic-low involvement group (a total of 73 in the intrinsic category), 19 respondents in the extrinsic-high involvement group, and 34 respondents in the extrinsic-low involvement group (a total of 53 in the extrinsic category). The total sample had 126 respondents; 55 were in the high-involved category, and 71 were in the low-involved category.

A two-way analysis of variance was performed on the composite mental health index of the respondents. The two main effects of job involvement ($F[1,122] = 7.43$, $p < .001$) and intrinsic orientation ($F[1,122] = 11.15$, $p < .001$) were statistically significant, but the interaction effect was not significant ($F[1,122] = 1.50, p > .05$). The mental health indexes for each of the four groups are presented in Figure 8.1. Visual inspection of Figure 8.1 makes it quite apparent that the intrinsic-low involved group had the highest composite mental health scores, and the extrinsic-high involved group had the lowest composite mental health scores. The mental health index of high- and low-involved categories and intrinsic and extrinsic categories were also calculated. The results, presented in Figure 8.2, clearly reveal the opposite relationship of the two variables with mental health.

Conclusion

It appears that greater involvement in one's job is associated with greater worry, anxiety, and apprehension concerning how the job needs to be done and whether the objectives will be attained. Psychological identification with the job may sensitize individuals to view even minor problems and failures on the job as matters too serious to be taken lightly. The resulting frustrations and tensions are, therefore, experienced too intensely. A strong affective experience of tension and frustration on the job may give rise to manifest hostility, which in turn may sometimes be directed toward one's own self (resulting in drug abuse, alcoholism, psychosomatic symptoms, and so on) and sometimes toward others (resulting in overt aggression and distrust).

While excessive job identification or job preoccupation is associated with poor mental health, an intrinsic job orientation is related to positive mental health. As was pointed out earlier, the concept of mental health tends to reflect cultural norms. The cultural norms of individualism in Western society (particularly in the United States and Canada) prescribe that people should strive for individual autonomy, independence, initiative, achievement, and personal success. Governed by such norms, people who strive for these goals in their lives are perceived as mentally healthy. Those who do not strive for these goals experience internal conflict between what they want for themselves and what the society wants them to be. Since intrinsic orientation in life is considered as an index of mental health (as measured by self-esteem and personal morale dimensions), it is quite natural that those who have an intrinsic job orientation would also be perceived to possess a positive mental health.

SUMMARY

The motivational approach to job and work involvement received considerable support from the results of the three studies reported in this chapter. The empirical validity of the conceptual distinction between job and work involvement is demonstrated in Studies I and II, using different measurement techniques. The criterion-related concurrent validity of newly developed measures of job and work involvement is established in Study II. The fundamental premise in the motivational approach regarding the distinctiveness and independence of job involvement and intrinsic motivational job orientation is empirically verified in all three of the studies. Overall, the studies not only support the motivational formulation but also question the validity of psychological and sociological theories of involvement and alienation currently in vogue.

9

DIRECTIONS FOR
FUTURE RESEARCH AND
APPLICATIONS

To arrive at some understanding of what is going on is
hard enough, without having also to meet the demand
that we anticipate what will happen next.

Abraham Kaplan, 1964

In this final chapter, let me recapitulate the two major purposes
of the book and then indicate some future research possibilities in the
area of job and work involvement. The first purpose of the book was
to critically examine the state of the art or our present understanding
of the phenomena of work alienation and involvement. This was done
in the first five chapters. A review of the literature on work alienation and involvement in these chapters revealed that the study of the
concepts and the phenomena they represent has a long history. The
concepts have come under the influence of both a rational and an empirical tradition. Such a long history and rich traditions provide a
clear indication of the importance attached to these concepts by philosophers and social scientists in their explanation of diverse social
phenomena. However, the same long history and rich traditions were
also responsible for giving the concepts varied meanings and consequently causing too much confusion in the current sociological and
psychological literature. Over a period of time the concepts became
equivocal, acquired excess meaning, and emerged surrounded by an
aura of mysticism. The sources in this confusion and mysticism in
the current literature were traced in the earlier chapters of the book,
and arguments were advanced in favor of the formulation of a new
approach to study work alienation and involvement.

The second purpose of the book was to provide a new conceptual
framework, called the motivational approach, for the study of work
alienation and involvement. This was done in Chapter 6. Several

implications of the motivational approach were tested in Chapters 7 and 8. There are two major advantages of the new motivational approach over the previous sociological and psychological formulations. First, the approach parsimoniously integrates the two parallel streams of sociological and psychological thinking on work alienation and involvement. Second, it provides a framework that has a broad cross-cultural generality. Some arguments and empirical evidences to prove the advantages of the motivational approach over the earlier approaches were presented; additional evidence in this regard awaits future research. However, in this final chapter it is necessary to make a few concluding remarks and some conjectural comments with respect to the potential of the motivational approach in directing future research and applications in the area of work alienation and involvement.

In order to bring about clarity in our understanding of the concepts of involvement and alienation, the motivational approach argues that the concepts should be distinguished from intrinsic motivation. All previous sociological and psychological formulations of the concepts and their operationalization have considered intrinsic motivation as a necessary precondition of work involvement and alienation. For this reason, studies based on the past formulations have produced ambiguous results with respect to the causes, effects, and correlates of involvement. These studies were reviewed in Chapters 3 and 4. In the empirical literature, an undue emphasis on the intrinsic motivation of workers as an essential precondition of involvement has resulted in a lack of attention to the role of extrinsic motivation. Researchers have consistently neglected or undermined the role of extrinsic motivation. Consequently, intrinsic job factors have assumed increasing importance in the job-design and quality-of-working life research accompanied by a total lack of concern for extrinsic job factors. For similar reasons, the selection, recruitment, and training procedures within organizations have been geared toward the search for and development of intrinsic orientation in available human resources. According to the motivational approach advocated in this book, these trends are reflections of a cultural bias introduced by Marx in his treatment of alienation and later adopted inadvertently by empirically oriented sociologists and psychologists. These trends, however, are in need of correction.

For a more accurate assessment of the psychological state of work involvement-alienation and its causes, effects, and correlates, the motivational approach argues that future studies should use the newly developed instruments presented in Chapter 7. These instruments are free of intrinsic bias and measure involvement-alienation as pure cognitive beliefs of psychological identification and separation. Measured this way the causes, effects, and correlates of involvement-alienation in different cultures and subcultures cannot only be accurately assessed but also meaningfully prepared. Furthermore, use of these instruments would help in assessing within any given culture the relative influence of intrinsic and extrinsic motivation on the state of involvement-alienation. The design of job or work settings based on such an assessment would be more effective in improving productivity and the quality of working life than the current practice of job design with a built-in bias toward meeting only the intrinsic needs of the workers.

The motivational approach also argues in favor of a clear distinction between involvement in a specific job and involvement with work in general. The former refers to a specific and descriptive belief of psychological identification with a given job, while the latter refers to a general and normative belief regarding the centrality of the work role in one's life. It is important that future research explore more fully the causes, effects, and correlates of the two kinds of beliefs. For instance, during a period of unemployment, a person who shows high work involvement may show greater dissatisfaction with living on unemployment insurance, may try harder to find jobs, and may show less reluctance for underemployment than a person who shows less work involvement. Job involvement, on the other hand, may not be related to these types of behavior. Job involvement should be more related to behavior on the specific job, such as the effort spent on the job or satisfaction with job outcomes.

Keeping this distinction between job and work involvement in mind, researchers should explore the nature of the causes of the two types of beliefs in different cultures. While job and work involvement may stem from the perceived potential of the job and work, respectively, to satisfy one's salient needs, the nature of these salient needs may differ from culture to culture. Thus, in one culture, Protestant-ethic socialization, with its emphasis on individualism, personal autonomy, and achievement, may be responsible for the development of a work ethic; in another culture, other forms of socialization, with an emphasis on collectivism, security, and affiliation, may cause the development of a work ethic. Perhaps in an individualistic society work derives its meaning and significance from its potential to satisfy personal success-oriented goals without any consideration for how it may or may not benefit others. In a collectivistic society, however, work assumes a moral value through serving a collectivistic purpose and has no meaning or importance without any reference to family, friends, and others.

There is also a need to explore how different salient needs of workers, be they intrinsic or extrinsic, determine job involvement in different cultures. In a culture that emphasizes individualism, workers' involvement in their jobs may primarily depend on the satisfaction of their salient needs for personal autonomy and control. This may not be true for workers belonging to a culture that values collectivism. These workers may develop job involvement through on-the-job satisfaction of their salient affiliative needs. Such culture-based differences in the nature of job involvement have obvious practical implications for job and organizational design and cross-cultural management. A uniform policy of organizational and job rewards may not be effective in producing greater job involvement among workers across cultures. Organizational and job outcomes that are viewed as rewarding in one culture may not be perceived as rewarding in another culture. This is the reason that job-design and organizational-development concepts developed in one culture (job enrichment, participative management, management by objectives, and so on developed in the United States) have questionable validity in other cultures. Some recent cross-national (Hofstede 1980) and cross-cultural (Kanungo 1980) studies provide considerable support to such a position.

Exploration into the nature of the relationship between job and work involvement in different cultures should be undertaken in the future. It would be of interest to identify conditions under which the two beliefs do or do not covary. It is quite conceivable that the relationship between the two beliefs may be affected by various social and physical conditions. For instance, at times of economic uncertainty (high unemployment, a tight job market, and so on) the two beliefs may covary, but under conditions of economic affluency they may not. Under conditions of economic uncertainty, individuals with high work involvement may show high job involvement in order to avoid the risk of being unemployed. This relationship may not be noticed when there are plenty of jobs available.

Researchers should also explore the relative contributions of historical and contemporary causes of the two beliefs. Although the normative belief of work involvement is conceived as being primarily historically conditioned, it is quite possible that such beliefs may undergo changes in one's lifetime as a result of contemporary influences. Individuals' normative beliefs, such as the work and family ethic, are maintained through social support and reinforcements they receive from time to time. Religious practices, educational training, or financial policies of the government (taxation, for example) have significant influences on maintenance of such beliefs. The nature and potency of such influences on work involvement need to be assessed.

Another interesting issue that requires further exploration is the relationship of the mental health of workers to their job involvement and motivational orientation. The problem of the mental health of workers is becoming more acute in modern organizations. Consequently, management's concern for creating appropriate job and organizational conditions that promote positive mental health is becoming increasingly important. In the past, management has assumed that highly motivated, job-involved workers tend to achieve career success and economic affluence because of their hard work and, as a result, enjoy a high degree of personal satisfaction in life and a positive mental health. As Korman and Korman (1980) pointed out, "Behaviorally, attitudinally, and philosophically, we have always been a society that promised great personal satisfaction for success based on materialistic acquisition and/or competitive supremacy" (p. 5). However, it is becoming increasingly apparent that occupational success and the economic affluency of workers does not necessarily contribute toward their positive mental health. Anecdotal and research evidence on managerial behavior has led Korman and Korman (1980) to propose that career success may, in fact, be related to personal failure and poor mental health. The realization that mental health problems may stem from career success makes it all the more necessary to understand how job involvement and motivational orientations (preconditions of career success) are related to mental health.

In the previous chapter, a study (Study III) dealing with the above issue was reported. The study revealed that the intrinsic motivational orientation of workers is positively related to mental health, whereas job involvement is negatively related to mental health. Such relationships raise some interesting possibilities for exploration in the areas of occupational stress and workaholism. For instance, stress researchers have classified people into two broad categories: those showing either "Type A" or "Type B" behavior (Friedman and Rosenman 1974). "Type A" individuals are characterized by such attributes as free-floating hostility, competitiveness, a high need for socially approved personal success or achievements, unbridled ambitions, aggressiveness, impatience, and polyphasic thought and action (striving to think of or do two or more things at the same time). "Type B" individuals are characterized by the opposite attributes. They are relaxed, patient, rarely harassed, and so on. In the working context, individual workers showing "Type A" behavior are characterized as having both intrinsic job orientation and high job involvement (Burke, Weir, and DuWors 1979). The results presented in Chapter 8 would suggest that the mental and physical health problems of these individuals are perhaps caused more by their excessive job involvement than their intrinsic orientation. There is also the interesting possibility of finding "Type A" behavior more among highly job-involved individuals who are extrinsically (seeking money, security, and so on) rather than intrinsically (seeking autonomy, respondibility, and so on) oriented. The common characterization of "Type A" persons as being both intrinsically oriented and highly job involved may have been a consequence of the past treatment of job involvement and intrinsic motivation as synonymous processes. In light of the results presented in Chapter 8, there is a strong possibility of finding strong extrinsic orientation among many "Type A" persons. This would also imply that the "Type B" category will include not only people with low job involvement but also people with intrinsic orientation.

These expectations are consistent with the description of "Type A" and "Type B" behavior by Friedman and Rosenman (1974). For instance, Friedman and Rosenman described the "Type A" person as one who has "a deep-seated insecurity" (p. 14), who "more often than not appears to be absorbed in money" (p. 90), and who wants to "capture the respect and admiration of his peers and superiors" (p. 91). The above three characteristics refer to extrinsic orientations (needs for security, money, and social recognition) of "Type A" persons. The "Type B" person, on the other hand, is described by Friedman and Rosenman (1974, p. 103) as one who "is far more aware of his capabilities than concerned about what peers and superiors may think of his action" and who finds "self-confidence by a process of candid self-appraisal." The above characteristics of "Type B" persons are indicative of their intrinsic orientation.

The motivational approach integrates the five variants of alienation suggested by sociologists (Seeman 1959) within its own framework. As discussed in Chapter 6, each type of alienation can be explained in motivational terms. The "isolation" type of job alienation results from the perceived lack of job potential to satisfy one's salient social or belonging needs. The "normlessness" type of job alienation results from the perceived lack of job potential to satisfy one's salient need for information. The "meaninglessness" and "powerlessness" types of alienation can result from the perceived lack of a job's potential to satisfy one's salient intrinsic needs for responsibility, autonomy, and control. Finally, a perceived lack of job opportunities to utilize one's valued abilities can result in the "self-estrangement" variant of alienation. Such psychological explanations of different types of alienation need to be empirically verified in future research. Since saliency of a specific type of need (affiliation, autonomy, achievement, and so on) is partly determined by cultural influences, it is quite possible that workers belonging to different cultures may exhibit different types of alienation. For instance, powerlessness and meaninglessness types of alienation may be a dominant theme in individualistic Western cultures, whereas the isolation type of alienation may be more common in collectivistic cultures in the East. Within a given society, different groups of people conditioned by their own subcultures may develop different salient needs; consequently, frustrations of these needs may lead them to experience different types of alienation. On the basis of the above reasoning, hypotheses regarding different types of alienation among various groups of workers (male/female, skilled/unskilled, management/labor, and so on) should be developed and tested in future studies.

Finally, the motivational approach may be helpful in exploring the nature of the relationship between one's involvement in work and nonwork spheres of life. Social philosophers and scientists (Champoux 1981; Cohen 1966; Dubin 1973; James 1891; Mead 1934) have argued that individuals' social lives are segmented and that they assume multiple social roles in different social settings, such as work, family, and community. Given this multiplicity of social roles, contemporary social scientists are very much interested in finding out how individuals' roles in work and nonwork contexts are interrelated. Sometimes it has been observed that work roles are central elements in one's life and, therefore, involvement-alienation in the work context can have a significant influence on the quality of life outside work (Wilensky 1961). Almost two centuries ago, Adam Smith (1937) observed that oversimplified factory jobs would cause workers to lose their skills and abilities and, consequently, would make them less effective in their nonwork roles in society. At other times, it has been argued that involvement-alienation at work is partly influenced by the quality of life one experiences in nonwork contexts. For instance, Friedmann (1960, 1961) observed that leisure activities in the nonwork sphere of life provide opportunities to reduce many adverse effects of job specialization. It is also a commonplace observation within work organizations that problems faced by workers in nonwork contexts have considerable influence on their job attitude and performance.

The relationship between individuals' roles in work and nonwork contexts has been described by three basic models (Champoux 1978, 1981; Parker 1971): spillover, compensatory, and no-relationship. According to the spillover model, beliefs, attitudes, values, and conditioned habits associated with the work role tend to generalize to other nonwork roles. Thus, the degree of involvement an individual has in work contexts should be positively related to the degree of involvement in other nonwork contexts, such as family and community. The compensatory model suggests just the opposite relationship. According to the compensatory model, alienation or noninvolvement in the work context should be compensated for by a high degree of involvement in the nonwork context. Hence, the relationship between involvement in work and nonwork contexts should be negative. The no-relationship model states that work and nonwork contexts are "physically, temporally and functionally segregated." Beliefs, attitudes, and behavior in one context may not necessarily be related to beliefs, attitudes, and behavior in another context (Champoux 1981; Dubin 1973; Meissner 1971). Thus, an individual's degree of involvement in work contexts should have no significant relationship to the degree of involvement in nonwork contexts.

The existing empirical literature does not provide conclusive evidence in support of any of these three alternative models. The reasons for our inconclusive knowledge in this area may stem from the theoretical and methodological problems identified earlier in this book. However, with the new motivational framework described in Chapters 6 and 7, systematic exploration of the validity of each of the models should be undertaken in the future.

Following the motivational approach, involvement in nonwork spheres of life, such as family and community, can be conceptualized as cognitive beliefs of psychological identification with these nonwork contexts. Instruments to measure these beliefs should be developed in a manner similar to that described in Chapter 7. It must be emphasized that in each of the nonwork contexts a distinction must be made between specific descriptive beliefs and general normative beliefs of involvement. For instance, with respect to one's involvement in the family context, the two types of beliefs must be distinguished: the specific descriptive belief of involvement with one's present family and the general normative belief regarding the centrality and moral value of the family institution in one's life. Viewed in this way, three networks of relationships among the beliefs need to be explored. First, one can explore the relationship among descriptive beliefs of involvement with one's present job and one's present family, community, and so on. Second, one can also explore the relationship among normative beliefs regarding the centrality and moral value of work, the family institution, the community, and so on in one's life. Finally, one can explore the relationship between a descriptive belief (such as job or present family involvement) and the corresponding belief (such as the centrality of work or the family institution). It is quite possible that the three networks of relationships may require different explanations. For instance, the compensatory model may best explain the relationship among specific descriptive beliefs of involvement with a present job, the family, and so on. Excessive job involvement may interfere with family involvement and vice versa. The same model, however, may not provide an appropriate explanation for the relationships between descriptive beliefs of involvement and the corresponding normative beliefs. Furthermore, it would be of interest to explore cross-cultural differences in the three sets of relationships. In a culture that promotes individualism, the relationships between involvement in work and nonwork roles may be very different from those observed in a culture that promotes collectivism.

The suggestions made in this chapter regarding directions for future research in the area of work alienation and involvement are more speculative than definitive. With a new theoretical framework and new measuring instruments, future research possibilities are numerous, and this discussion of the issues has only touched on a few of them.

APPENDIX A

OLD MEASURES

I. Items from the Blood (1969) Work-Values Scale

Protestant-Ethic Items:

1. Hard work makes a man a better person.
2. Wasting time is as bad as wasting money.
3. A good indication of a man's worth is how well he does his job.
4. If all other things are equal, it is better to have a job with a lot of responsibility than one with little responsibility.

Non-Protestant-Ethic Items:

5. When the workday is finished, a person should forget his job and enjoy himself.
6. The principal purpose of a man's job is to provide him with the means for enjoying his free time.
7. Whenever possible a person should relax and accept life as it is, rather than always striving for unreachable goals.
8. People who "do things the easy way" are the smart ones.

II. Items from the Lodahl and Kejner (1965) Job-Involvement Scale

1. I'll stay overtime to finish a job, even if I'm not paid for it.
2. You can measure a person pretty well by how good a job he does.
3. The major satisfaction in my life comes from my job.
4. For me, mornings at work really fly by.
5. I usually show up for work a little early to get things ready.
6. The most important things that happen to me involve my work.
7. Sometimes I lie awake at night thinking ahead to the next day's work.
8. I'm really a perfectionist about my work.
9. I feel depressed when I fail at something connected with my job.
10. I have other activities more important than my work.
11. I live, eat, and breathe my job.

12. I would probably keep working even if I didn't need the money.
13. Quite often I feel like staying home from work instead of coming in.
14. To me, my work is only a small part of who I am.
15. I am very much involved personally in my work.
16. I avoid taking on extra duties and responsibilities in my work.
17. I used to be more ambitious about my work than I am now.
18. Most things in life are more important than work.
19. I used to care more about my work, but now other things are more important to me.
20. Sometimes I'd like to kick myself for the mistakes I make in my work.

(Items 3, 6, 8, 11, 15, and 18 are included in the short version of the scale.)

III. Items from the Saleh and Hosek (1976) Job-Involvement Scale

Active Participation Items:

1. How much chance do you get to use the skills you have learned for your job?
2. How much chance do you get to do things your own way?
3. How much chance do you get to try out your own ideas?
4. How much chance do you get to do the kinds of things you are best at?
5. How much chance do you get to do interesting work?
6. How much chance do you get to feel at the end of the day that you've accomplished something?
7. How much chance do you get to learn new things?
8. In general, I have much say and influence over what goes on in my job.
9. How much chance do you get to finish things?
10. My immediate superior asks my opinion when a problem comes up which involves my work.
11. How much chance do you get to work without feeling pushed?
12. If I have a suggestion for improving the job or setup in some way, it is easy for me to get my ideas across to my immediate superior.
13. I have a chance to make important decisions on my job.
14. I feel I can influence the decisions of my immediate superior regarding the things about which I am concerned.

Central Life-Interest Items:

15. The most important things that happen to me involve my work.
16. The most important things I do are involved with my job.
17. The major satisfaction in my life comes from my job.
18. The activities which give me the greatest pleasure and personal satisfaction involve my job.
19. I live, eat, and breathe my job.
20. The most important things I do concern my job.
21. I enjoy my work more than anything else that I do.
22. I have other activities more important than my work.
23. To me, work is only a small part of who I am.
24. I enjoy keeping my work space in good shape more than keeping my things around the house in good shape.

Self-Esteem Items:

25. How well I perform on my job is extremely important to me.
26. I feel badly if I don't perform well on my job.
27. I am very much personally involved in my work.
28. I avoid taking on extra duties and responsibilities in my work.
29. I feel good when I perform my job well.
30. I am able to utilize abilities I value in the performance of my job.

IV. Items from the Shepard (1971) Work-Alienation Scales *

Items Measuring Powerlessness in Work:

1. To what extent can you vary the steps involved in doing your job?
2. To what extent can you move from your immediate working area during work hours?
3. To what extent can you control how much work you produce?
4. To what extent can you help decide on methods and procedures used in your job?
5. To what extent do you have influence over the things that happen to you at work?
6. To what extent can you do your work ahead and take a short rest break during work hours?
7. To what extent are you free from close supervision while doing your job?
8. To what extent can you increase the speed at which you do your work?

*Material from Shephard (1971) used by permission of MIT Press.

Items Measuring Meaninglessness in Work:

1. To what extent do you know how your job fits into the total plant (operations of the company)?
2. To what extent do you know how your job fits in with the work of other departments in the plant (company)?
3. To what extent do you know how your work relates to the work of others that you work with?

Items Measuring Normlessness in Work:

1. To what extent do you feel that people who get ahead in the plant (company) deserve it?
2. To what extent do you feel that it is pull and connection that gets a person ahead in the plant (company)?
3. To what extent is getting ahead in the plant (company) based on ability?

Items Measuring Instrumental Work Orientation:

1. Your job is something you have to do to earn a living; most of your real interests are centered outside your job (occupation).
2. Money is the most rewarding reason for working.
3. Working is a necessary evil to provide things your family and you want.
4. You are living for the day when you can collect your retirement and do the things that are important to you.

Items Measuring Self-Evaluative Involvement in the Work Role:

1. Success in the things you do away from the job is more important to your opinion of yourself than success in your work (occupational) career.
2. To you, your work (occupation) is only a small part of who you are.

V. Items from the Warr, Cook, and Wall (1979) Work-Involvement Scale

1. Even if I won a great deal of money on the pools I would continue to work somewhere.
2. Having a job is very important to me.
3. I should hate to be on the dole.
4. I would soon get very bored if I had no work to do.
5. The most important things that happen to me involve work.
6. If unemployment benefit was really high I would still prefer to work.

APPENDIX B

NEW MEASURES

QUESTIONNAIRE USED FOR DEVELOPING
NEW SCALES OF JOB AND WORK INVOLVEMENT

I. Measure of Perceived Importance of Job Outcomes

INSTRUCTIONS

Below is a list of things people look for in their job career.
Please read all the items from top to bottom before making any choice.
First decide which one you think is the most important to you in your
present job and then place 1 in the blank provided for the item. Do
the same for your choice 2, 3, 4, 5, and so on. Since there are 15
items in the list given below, your choice 15 would represent the
thing that is least important to you in your present job. Please be
sure you have placed a number opposite each item.

____Security (permanent job, steady work)
____Adequate earning (for a better standard of living)
____Benefits (vacations, bonus, pension, insurance, profit sharing,
medical benefits, disability, dental benefits, and so on
____Opportunity for future promotion
____Comfortable working conditions (pleasant surrounding, good light-
ing, air conditioning, good office space, and so on)
____Interesting nature of work (a job that you very much enjoy)
____Sound company policies and practices (reasonable and nondiscrim-
inatory)
____Respect and recognition (from superiors and coworkers for your
work)
____Responsibility and independence (a job that gives you responsibil-
ity to work in your own way)
____Achievement (opportunity to achieve excellence in your work)
____Good interpersonal relations (a job that gives you the opportunity
to work with others whom you like)
____Considerate and sympathetic superior
____Technically competent superior
____Opportunity for professional growth (to become more skilled and
competent on the job)
____Fair pay for the work you do

II. Measures of Job Satisfaction

INSTRUCTIONS

In this part are listed some job characteristics or qualities that people look for in their jobs. We would like to know the degree of your satisfaction or dissatisfaction with each of the job qualities as they relate to your present job. For each job quality listed below, you will find six answer categories. Please indicate your feeling by putting a cross (X) mark in the appropriate space representing your answer. Make sure that you indicate your feelings for each item.

	6	5	4	3	2	1
	Extremely Satisfied	Moderately Satisfied	Mildly Satisfied	Mildly Dissatisfied	Moderately Disssatisfied	Extremely Dissatisfied
1. With the amount of security I have on my job, I feel	___	___	___	___	___	___
2. With the kind of company policies and practices that govern my job, I feel	___	___	___	___	___	___
3. With the amount of compensation that I receive to maintain a reasonably good living, I feel	___	___	___	___	___	___
4. With the kind of benefit plans (vacation, retirement, medical, and so on) that go with my job, I feel	___	___	___	___	___	___
5. With the chance of future promotion I have in my job, I feel	___	___	___	___	___	___

| | 6 | 5 | 4 | 3 | 2 | 1 |
	Extremely Satisfied	Moderately Satisfied	Mildly Satisfied	Mildly Dissatisfied	Moderately Dissatisfied	Extremely Dissatisfied
6. With the kind of working conditions (lighting, noise, office space, and so on) surrounding my job, I feel	—	—	—	—	—	—
7. With the interesting or enjoyable nature of the work in my job, I feel	—	—	—	—	—	—
8. With the amount of recognition and respect that I receive for my work, I feel	—	—	—	—	—	—
9. With the opportunity I have in my job to work with people I like, I feel	—	—	—	—	—	—
10. With the technical competence of my immediate superior, I feel	—	—	—	—	—	—
11. With the opportunity that I have in my job to achieve excellence in my work, I feel	—	—	—	—	—	—
12. With the considerate and sympathetic nature of my immediate superior, I feel	—	—	—	—	—	—
13. With the kind of responsibility and independence that I have in my job, I feel	—	—	—	—	—	—

	6	5	4	3	2	1
	Extremely Satisfied	Moderately Satisfied	Mildly Satisfied	Mildly Dissatisfied	Moderately Dissatisfied	Extremely Dissatisfied

14. With the opportunity for acquiring higher skill, I feel ___ ___ ___ ___ ___ ___

15. With the amount of compensation I receive for the work I do, I feel ___ ___ ___ ___ ___ ___

16. From an overall consideration, with respect to my job, I feel ___ ___ ___ ___ ___ ___

III. Measures of Job Involvement

A. Semantic-Differential Format (JISD)

INSTRUCTIONS

Think about your present job in the context of your life and evaluate it using each of the seven-point scales presented below. Circle the number in each scale which most closely describes your attitude toward your present job.

To me, my present job is:

a.	Involving	1	2	3	4	5	6	7	Noninvolving
b.	Important	1	2	3	4	5	6	7	Unimportant
c.	Unmotivating	1	2	3	4	5	6	7	Motivating
d.	Fundamental	1	2	3	4	5	6	7	Trivial
e.	Unrewarding	1	2	3	4	5	6	7	Rewarding
f.	Essential	1	2	3	4	5	6	7	Nonessential

In relation to my present job, I am:

g.	Identified	1	2	3	4	5	6	7	Not identified
h.	Attached	1	2	3	4	5	6	7	Detached
i.	Bored	1	2	3	4	5	6	7	Excited
j.	Integrated	1	2	3	4	5	6	7	Nonintegrated
k.	Dissatisfied	1	2	3	4	5	6	7	Satisfied
l.	United	1	2	3	4	5	6	7	Disunited

(Items c, e, i, and k are filler items.)

B. Questionnaire Format (JIQ)

INSTRUCTIONS

Below are a number of statements each of which you may agree or disagree with depending on your own personal evaluation of your present job. Please indicate the degree of your agreement or disagreement with each statement by putting a cross (X) mark in one of the six blanks representing the answer categories (strongly agree; agree; mildly agree; mildly disagree; disagree; strongly disagree) that appear against the statement.

Statements	Answer Categories					
	Strongly Agree	Agree	Mildly Agree	Mildly Disagree	Disagree	Strongly Disagree
a. The most important things that happen to me involve my present job	____	____	____	____	____	____
b. I'll stay overtime to finish my job, even if I'm not paid for it	____	____	____	____	____	____
c. To me, my job is only a small part of who I am	____	____	____	____	____	____
d. I am very much involved personally in my job	____	____	____	____	____	____
e. Generally I avoid taking on extra duties and responsibilities in my job	____	____	____	____	____	____
f. I live, eat, and breathe my job	____	____	____	____	____	____
g. Sometimes I'd like to kick myself for the mistakes I make in my job	____	____	____	____	____	____
h. Most of my interests are centered around my job	____	____	____	____	____	____

		Strongly Agree	Agree	Mildly Agree	Mildly Disagree	Disagree	Strongly Disagree

Answer Categories

i.   I have very strong ties with my present job which would be very difficult to break ___ ___ ___ ___ ___ ___

j.   Usually I feel detached from my job ___ ___ ___ ___ ___ ___

k.   Most of my personal life goals are job-oriented ___ ___ ___ ___ ___ ___

l.   I feel depressed when I fail at something connected with my job ___ ___ ___ ___ ___ ___

m.   I consider my job to be very central to my existence ___ ___ ___ ___ ___ ___

n.   I have other activities which are more satisfying than my job ___ ___ ___ ___ ___ ___

o.   I like to be absorbed in my job most of the time ___ ___ ___ ___ ___ ___

(Items b, e, g, l, and n are filler items.)

C. Graphic Format (JIG)

To the right are seven boxes, each containing two circles. One circle represents your present job and the other circle represents yourself. The circles overlap in various degrees. At one extreme, (box 1) the two circles are separate, representing you being separate from your present job. At the other extreme, (box 7) the two circles are totally overlapping, representing you being totally involved in your present job. Select the box which most accurately depicts your relationship to your present job and circle the appropriate number.

Below are seven diagrams. In each diagram there is a person, representing yourself and a desk, representing your present job. The figures are placed at different distances from each other, depicting how close or how far one is from one's job. Distance in the diagram does not represent physical distance from the job. Instead, being close to one's job implies that the job is central to one's life and being far from one's job implies that the job is not central to one's life. In your opinion, how far are you from your present job. Circle the appropriate number.

171

IV. Measures of Work Involvement

A. Semantic-Differential Format (WISD)

INSTRUCTIONS

The value placed on work in general in life (without reference to any specific job) varies from individual to individual. Think about the role of work in your life (without reference to your present job) and evaluate it using each of the seven-point scales presented below. Circle the number in each scale which most closely describes your attitude toward work in general.

To me, work in general is:

a.	Involving	1	2	3	4	5	6	7	Noninvolving
b.	Important	1	2	3	4	5	6	7	Unimportant
c.	Unimportant	1	2	3	4	5	6	7	Motivating
d.	Fundamental	1	2	3	4	5	6	7	Trivial
e.	Unrewarding	1	2	3	4	5	6	7	Rewarding
f.	Essential	1	2	3	4	5	6	7	Nonessential

In relation to work in general, I am:

g.	Identified	1	2	3	4	5	6	7	Not identified
h.	Attached	1	2	3	4	5	6	7	Detached
i.	Bored	1	2	3	4	5	6	7	Excited
j.	Integrated	1	2	3	4	5	6	7	Nonintegrated
k.	Dissatisfied	1	2	3	4	5	6	7	Satisfied
l.	United	1	2	3	4	5	6	7	Disunited

(Items c, e, i, and k are filler items.)

B. Questionnaire Format (WIQ)

INSTRUCTIONS

Below are a number of statements each of which you may agree or disagree with depending on your own personal evaluation of work in general without reference to your present job. Please indicate the degree of your agreement or disagreement with each statement by putting a cross (X) mark in one of the six blanks representing the answer categories (strongly agree; agree; mildly agree; mildly disagree; disagree; strongly disagree) that appear against the statement.

Statements	Answer Categories					
	Strongly Agree	Agree	Mildly Agree	Mildly Disagree	Disagree	Strongly Disagree
a. The most important things that happen in life involve work	___	___	___	___	___	___
b. Work is something people should get involved in most of the time	___	___	___	___	___	___
c. Work should be only a small part of one's life	___	___	___	___	___	___
d. Happiness in life comes mainly through work	___	___	___	___	___	___
e. People feel guilty if they don't work	___	___	___	___	___	___
f. Work should be considered central to life	___	___	___	___	___	___
g. There are other activities which are more meaningful than work	___	___	___	___	___	___
h. In my view, an individual's personal life goals should be work-oriented	___	___	___	___	___	___
i. Work should be a fulfilling experience	___	___	___	___	___	___
j. Life is worth living only when people get absorbed in work	___	___	___	___	___	___
k. People should derive satisfaction from work	___	___	___	___	___	___

(Items d, e, g, i, and k are filler items.)

C. Graphic Format (WIG)

To the right are seven boxes, each containing two circles. One circle represents work in general and the other circle represents yourself. The circles overlap in various degrees. At one extreme, (box 1) the two circles are separate, representing you being separate from work in general. At the other extreme, (box 7) the two circles are totally overlapping, representing you being totally involved in work in general.

Select the box which most accurately depicts your relationship to work in general and circle the appropriate number.

INSTRUCTIONS

Below are seven diagrams. In each diagram there is a person, representing yourself and a desk, representing work in general. The figures are placed at different distances from each other, depicting how close or how far one is from work in general. Distance in the diagram does not represent physical distance from work in general. Instead, being close to work in general implies that work in general is central to one's life and being far from work in general implies that work in general is not central to one's life. In your opinion, how far are you from work in general? Circle the appropriate number.

174

V. Measures of Demographic Variables

INSTRUCTIONS

Please make a check (√) mark in the appropriate space against the information applicable to you and fill in the necessary information in the space provided below.

What is your sex?

_____male
_____female

What is your present age in years?   _____years

What is your present marital status?

_____married
_____single
_____divorced or separated
_____engaged to be married

Indicate the language spoken in your home

_____French
_____English
_____both
other_____

Indicate your mother tongue

_____French
_____English
_____both
other _____

How many years have you been residing in Canada? _____years

How many years have you been residing in Quebec? _____years

Indicate your highest attained level of formal education.

_____some high school
_____high school graduation
_____some college
_____college degree
_____some graduate study
_____advanced degree

What is the nature of the organization you represent?

_____public sector
_____private sector

What is the size of your organization?

_____small (less than 200 employees)
_____medium (200–700 employees)
_____large (over 700 employees)

How long have you been serving in the organization? _____

What is your present job title? _____

How long have you been in your present position? _____

What is your present salary?

_____less than $19,999 per year
_____$20,000–$29,999
_____$30,000–$39,999
_____$40,000–$49,999
_____more than $50,000

REFERENCES

Aldag, R. J., and A. F. Brief. 1975. "Some Correlates of Work Values." Journal of Applied Psychology 60: 757-60.

Alderfer, C. P. 1972. Existence, Relatedness, Growth: Human Needs in Organizational Settings. New York: Free Press.

Alderfer, C. P., and T. M. Lodahl. 1971. "A Quasi Experiment on the Use of Experimental Methods in the Classroom." Journal of Applied Behavioral Science 7: 43-69.

Allport, G. W. 1961. Pattern and Growth in Personality. New York: Holt, Rinehart and Winston.

_____. 1947. "The Psychology of Participation." Psychological Review 52: 117-32.

Aonuma, Y. 1981. "A Japanese Explains Japan's Business Style." Across the Board, (February), pp. 41-50.

Argyris, C. 1964. Integrating the Individual and the Organization. New York: Wiley.

Auclair, G. A., and W. H. Read. 1966. A Cross-cultural Study of Industrial Leadership. Royal Commission on Bilingualism and Biculturalism Report, vol. 2. Ottawa: Government of Canada.

Baba, V. V. 1979. "Job Involvement: A Critical Review." Working Paper Series, Concordia University, Montreal. Mimeographed.

Baba, V. V., and M. Jamal. 1976. "On the Nature of Company Satisfaction, Company Commitment and Work Involvement: An Empirical Examination of Blue-Collar Workers." Relations industrielles 31: 434-47.

Bass, B. M. 1965. Organizational Psychology. Boston: Allyn and Bacon.

Bass, B. M., and G. V. Barrett. 1972. Man, Work and Organizations. Boston: Allyn and Bacon.

Becker, H. S., and J. Carper. 1956. "The Elements of Identification with an Occupation." American Sociological Review 21: 341–47.

Beehr, T. A., and N. Gupta. 1978. "A Note on the Structure of Employee Withdrawal." Organizational Behavior and Human Performance 21: 73-79.

Bigoness, W. J. 1978. "Correlates of Faculty Attitudes toward Collective Bargaining." Journal of Applied Psychology 63: 228-33.

Blauner, R. 1964. Alienation and Freedom: The Factory Worker and His Industry. Chicago: University of Chicago Press.

Blood, M. R. 1969. "Work Values and Job Satisfaction." Journal of Applied Psychology 33: 456-59.

Blood, M. R., and C. Hulin. 1967. "Alienation, Environmental Characteristics and Worker Responses." Journal of Applied Psychology 51: 284-90.

Bradburn, N. M., and D. Caplovitz. 1965. Reports on Happiness: A Pilot Study of Behavior Related to Mental Health. Chicago: Aldine Press.

Brief, A. P., R. J. Aldag, and R. A. Wallden. 1976. "Correlates of Supervisory Style among Policemen." Criminal Justice and Behavior 3: 263-71.

Buchanan, B., II. 1974. "Building Organizational Commitment: The Socialization of Managers in Work Organizations." Administrative Science Quarterly 19: 533-46.

Burke, R. J., T. Weir, and R. E. DuWors. 1979. "Type A Behavior of Administrators and Wives' Reports of Marital Satisfaction and Well-Being." Journal of Applied Psychology 64: 57-65.

Calvin, J. 1854. Commentaries on the Epistles of Paul to the Galatians and Ephesians, translated by William Pringle. Edinburgh: Calvin Translation Society.

Campbell, D. T., and D. W. Fiske. 1959. "Convergent and Discriminant Validation by the Multitrait-Multimethod Matrix." Psychological Bulletin 56: 81-105.

Champoux, J. E. 1981. "A Sociological Perspective on Work Involvement." International Review of Applied Psychology 30: 65-86.

_____. 1978. "Perceptions of Work and Nonwork: A Reexamination of the Compensatory and Spillover Models." Sociology of Work and Occupations 5: 402-22.

Chatterjee, A., and A. Ganguly. 1977. "Differential Perception of Certain Industry-Related Concepts by Two Groups of Managers." Indian Journal of Industrial Relations 13: 235-41.

Cherrington, D. J. 1977. "The Value of Younger Workers." Business Horizon 20: 18-30.

Cherrington, D. J., S. J. Condie, and J. L. England. 1979. "Age and Work Values." Academy of Management Journal 22: 617-23.

Chung, K. H., and L. C. Megginson. 1981. Organizational Behavior: Developing Managerial Skills. New York: Harper & Row.

Clark, J. P. 1959. "Measuring Alienation within a Social System." American Sociological Review 24: 849-52.

Cleland, V., A. R. Bass, W. McHugh, and J. Montano. 1976. "Social and Psychological Influences on Employment of Married Nurses." Nursing Research 25: 90-97.

Cohen, P. S. 1966. "Social Attitudes and Sociological Enquiry." British Journal of Sociology 17: 341-52.

Cook, T. D., and D. T. Campbell. 1976. "The Design and Conduct of Quasi-Experiments and True Experiments in Field Settings." In Handbook of Industrial and Organizational Psychology, edited by Marvin D. Dunnette, pp. 223-326. Chicago: Rand McNally.

Cummings, L. L., and D. P. Schwab. 1973. Performance in Organizations: Determinants and Appraisal. Glenview, Ill.: Scott, Foresman.

Cummings, T. G., and S. L. Mauring. 1977. "Relationship between Worker Alienation and Work Related Behavior." Journal of Vocational Behavior 10: 167-79.

Davis, J. W., Jr. 1966. "Work Involvement of Executives." Personnel Administration 29: 6-12.

Dean, D. G. 1961. "Alienation: Its Meaning and Measurement." American Sociological Review 26: 753-58.

Denise, T. C. 1973. "The Concept of Alienation: Some Critical Notices." In Alienation: Concept, Term, and Meanings, edited by Frank Johnson, pp. 141-60. New York: Seminar Press.

Dubin, R. 1973. "Work and Non-Work: Institutional Perspectives." In Work and Non-Work in the Year 2001, edited by M. D. Dunnette, pp. 53-68. Monterey, Calif.: Brook/Cole.

_____. 1956. "Industrial Workers' Worlds: A Study of the Central Life Interests of Industrial Workers." Social Problems 3: 131-42.

Dubin, R., J. E. Champoux, and L. W. Porter. 1975. "Central Life Interests and Organizational Commitment of Blue Collar and Clerical Workers." Administrative Science Quarterly 20: 411-21.

Duncan, O. D. 1961. "A Socioeconomic Index for All Occupations, and Properties and Characteristics of the Socioeconomic Index." In Occupations and Social Status, edited by A. J. Reiss, Jr., O. D. Duncan, P. K. Hatt, and C. C. North, pp. 109-61. New York: Free Press.

Dunne, E. J., Jr., M. J. Stahl, and L. J. Melhart, Jr. 1978. "Influence Sources of Project and Functional Managers in Matrix Organizations." Academy of Management Journal 21: 135-40.

Durkheim, E. 1893. De la division du travail social. Paris: F. Alcan.

Edwards, J. E., and L. K. Waters. 1980. "Academic Job Involvement: Multiple Measures and Their Correlates." Psychological Reports 47: 1263-66.

England, G. W., and R. Lee. 1974. "The Relationship between Managerial Values and Managerial Success in the U.S., Japan, India, and Australia." Journal of Applied Psychology 59: 411-19.

Etzioni, A. 1968. "Basic Human Needs: Alienation and Inauthenticity." American Sociological Review 33: 870-85.

Farris, G. F. 1971. "A Predictive Study of Turnover." Personnel Psychology 24: 311-28.

Faunce, W. A. 1968. Problems of an Industrial Society. New York: McGraw-Hill.

_____. 1959. "Occupational Involvement and Selective Testing of Self-Esteem." Paper presented at the American Sociological Association Meeting in Chicago.

Festinger, L. 1954. "A Theory of Social Comparison Processes." Human Relations 7: 117-40.

French, J. R. P., Jr. 1963. "The Social Environment and Mental Health." Journal of Social Issues 19 (October): 39-56.

French, J. R. P., Jr., and R. Kahn. 1962. "A Programmatic Approach to Studying the Industrial Environment and Mental Health." Journal of Social Issues 18: 1-47.

Friedlander, F., and N. Margulies. 1969. "Multiple Impacts of Organizational Climate and Individual Value Systems upon Job Satisfaction." Personnel Psychology 22: 171-83.

Friedman, M., and R. H. Rosenman. 1974. Type B Behavior and Your Heart. Greenwich, Conn.: Fawcett.

Friedmann, G. 1961. The Anatomy of Work: New York: Free Press.

_____. 1960. "Leisure and Technological Civilization." International Social Science Journal 12: 509-21.

Fromm, E. 1966. Marx's Concept of Man. New York: Frederick Ungar.

_____. 1941. Escape from Freedom. New York: Avon.

Gadbois, C. 1971. "L'implication dans le travail a l'entrée en apprentissage structure et déterminants." Travail humaine 34: 277-78.

Gannon, M. J., and D. H. Hendrickson. 1973. "Career Orientation and Job Satisfaction among Working Wives." Journal of Applied Psychology 57: 339-40.

Gardell, B. 1977. "Autonomy and Participation at Work." Human Relations 30: 515-33.

Gechman, A. S., and Y. Wiener. 1975. "Job Involvement and Satisfaction Related to Mental Health and Personal Time Devoted to Work." Journal of Applied Psychology 60: 521-23.

Gerth, H. H., and C. W. Mills. 1946. From Max Weber: Essays in Sociology. New York: Oxford University Press.

Geyer, R. F., ed. 1974. Bibliography Alienation. Supplement to the 2nd ed. Amsterdam: Netherlands Universities' Joint Social Research Centre.

_____. 1972. Bibliography Alienation. Amsterdam: Netherlands Universities' Joint Social Research Centre.

Goldthorpe, J. H. 1966. "Attitudes and Behavior of Car Assembly Workers: A Deviant Case and a Theoretical Critique." British Journal of Sociology 17: 227-44.

Goldthorpe, J. H., D. Lockwood, F. Bechhofer, and J. Platt. 1968. The Affluent Worker: Industrial Attitudes and Behavior. Cambridge: At the University Press.

Goodman, P. S., J. H. Rose, and J. E. Furcon. 1970. "Comparison of Motivational Antecedents of the Work Performance of Scientists and Engineers." Journal of Applied Psychology 54: 491-95.

Gorn, G. J., and R. N. Kanungo. 1980. "Job Involvement and Motivation: Are Intrinsically Motivated Managers More Job Involved?" Organizational Behavior and Human Performance 26: 265-77.

Grotius, H. 1853. De jure belli ac pacis. Translated by W. Whewell. London: John W. Parker.

Gurin, G., J. Veroff, and S. Feld. 1960. Americans View Their Mental Health. New York: Basic Books.

Hackman, J. R., and G. R. Oldham. 1976. "Motivation through the Design of Work: Test of a Theory." Organizational Behavior and Human Performance 16: 250-79.

Hall, D. T., and L. W. Foster. 1977. "A Psychological Success Cycle and Goal Setting: Goals, Performance and Attitudes." Academy of Management Journal 20: 282-90.

Hall, D. T., J. G. Goodale, S. Rabinowitz, and M. A. Morgan. 1978. "Effects of Top-Down Departmental and Job Change upon Perceived Employee Behavior and Attitudes: A Natural Field Experiment." Journal of Applied Psychology 63: 62-72.

Hall, D. T., and F. S. Hall. 1976. "The Relationship between Goals, Performance, Success, Self-image and Involvement under Different Organization Climates." Journal of Vocational Behavior 9: 276-98.

Hall, D. T., and E. E. Lawler. 1970. "Job Characteristics and Pressures and the Integration of Professionals." Administrative Science Quarterly 15: 271-81.

Hall, D. T., and R. Mansfield. 1975. "Relationships of Age and Seniority with Career Variables of Engineers and Scientists." Journal of Applied Psychology 60: 201-10.

Hall, D. T., and B. Schneider. 1972. "Correlates of Organizational Identification as a Function of Career Pattern and Organization Type." Administrative Science Quarterly 17: 340-50.

Hall, D. T., B. Schneider, and H. T. Nygren. 1970. "Personal Factors in Organizational Identification." Administrative Science Quarterly 15: 176-90.

Hegel, G. W. F. 1949. Phenomenology of Mind, translated by J. B. Baillie. New York: Macmillan.

_____. 1942. Philosophy of Right, translated by T. M. Knox. Oxford: Clarendon.

Herman, J. B., R. B. Dunham, and C. L. Hulin. 1975. "Organizational Structure, Demographic Characteristics and Employee Responses." Organizational Behavior and Human Performance 13: 206-32.

Herzberg, F. 1968. "One More Time: How Do You Motivate Employees?" Harvard Business Review 46 (January-February): 53-62.

_____. 1966. Work and the Nature of Man. Cleveland, Ohio: World.

Hobbes, T. 1950. Leviathan. New York: E. P. Dutton.

Hofstede, G. 1980. Culture's Consequences: National Differences in Thinking and Organizing. Beverly Hills, Calif.: Sage.

Hollon, C. J., and R. J. Chesser. 1976. "The Relationship of Personal Influence Dissonance to Job Tension, Satisfaction and Involvement." Academy of Management Journal 19: 308-14.

Hollon, C. J., and G. R. Gemmill. 1976. "A Comparison of Female and Male Professors on Participation in Decision Making, Job Related Tension, Job Involvement and Job Satisfaction." Educational Administration Quarterly 12: 80-93.

House, R. J. 1971. "A Path-Goal Theory of Leader Effectiveness." Administrative Science Quarterly 16: 321-28.

Hulin, C. J. 1972. "Industrial Differences and Job Enrichment: The Case against General Treatment." In Organizational Issues in Industrial Society, edited by J. M. Shepard, pp. 387-410. Englewood Cliffs, N.J.: Prentice-Hall.

Hulin, C. L., and M. Blood. 1968. "Job Enlargement, Individual Differences and Worker Responses." Psychological Bulletin 69: 41-55.

Inkson, K., and D. Simpson. 1975. "The Assembly-Line and Alienation: A Participant-Observer Study in the Meat-Freezing Industry." New Zealand Psychologist 4: 44-55.

Ivancevish, J. M., and J. T. McMahon. 1977. "A Study of Task-Goal Attributes, Higher Order Need Strength and Performance." Academy of Management Journal 20: 552-63.

Iverson, M. A., and M. E. Reuder. 1956. "Ego Involvement as an Experimental Variable." Psychological Reports 2: 147-81.

Jahoda, M. 1958. Current Concepts of Positive Mental Health. New York: Basic Books.

Jain, H. C., J. Normand, and R. N. Kanungo. 1979. "Job Motivation of Canadian Anglophone and Francophone Hospital Employees." Canadian Journal of Behavioral Science 11: 160-63.

Jamal, M., T. Barnowe, and V. Mitchell. 1977. "Surveying Workers' Mental Health: Aspirin for Measurement Headache." Paper presented at the American Psychological Association Meeting in San Francisco.

Jamal, M., and V. F. Mitchell. 1980. "Work, Non-Work, and Mental Health: A Model and a Test." Industrial Relations 19: 88-93.

James, W. 1891. The Principles of Psychology, vol. 1. London: Macmillan.

Jenkins, D. 1973. Job Power. New York: Doubleday.

Johnson, F. 1973. "Alienation: An Overview and Introduction." In Alienation: Concepts, Terms, and Meanings, edited by Frank Johnson, pp. 3-25. New York: Seminar Press.

Johnson, F. 1973. "Alienation: Concept, Term, and Word." In Alienation: Concepts, Terms, and Meanings, edited by Frank Johnson, pp. 27-51. New York: Seminar Press.

Jones, A. P., L. R. James, and J. R. Bruni. 1975. "Perceived Leadership Behavior and Employee Confidence in the Leader as Moderated by Job Involvement." Journal of Applied Psychology 60: 146-49.

Jones, A. P., L. R. James, J. R. Bruni, and S. B. Sells. 1977. "Black-White Differences in Work Environment Perceptions and Job Satisfaction and Its Correlates." Personnel Psychology 30: 5-16.

Jones, E. E., and H. B. Gerard. 1967. Foundations of Social Psychology. New York: Wiley.

Josephson, E., and R. Josephson. 1973. "Alienation: Contemporary Sociological Approaches." In Alienation: Concepts, Terms, and Meanings, edited by Frank Johnson, pp. 163-80. New York: Seminar Press.

Kanungo, R. N. 1981. "Work Alienation and Involvement: Problems and Prospects." International Review of Applied Psychology 30: 1-16.

_____. 1980. Biculturalism and Management. Toronto: Butterworths.

_____. 1979. "The Concepts of Alienation and Involvement Revisited." Psychological Bulletin 86: 119-38.

_____. 1977. "Bases of Supervisory Power and Job Satisfaction in a Bicultural Context." In Behavioral Issues in Management: The Canadian Context, edited by H. C. Jain and R. N. Kanungo, pp. 331-44. Toronto: McGraw-Hill Ryerson.

Kanungo, R. N., G. J. Gorn, and H. J. Dauderis. 1976. "Motivational Orientation of Canadian Anglophone and Francophone Managers." Canadian Journal of Behavioral Science 8: 107-21.

Kanungo, R. N., S. B. Misra, and I. Dayal. 1975. "Relationship of Job Involvement to Perceived Importance and Satisfaction of Employee Needs." International Review of Applied Psychology 24: 39-59.

Kanungo, R. N., and R. W. Wright. 1981. "A Cross-cultural Comparative Study of Managerial Job Attitudes." Paper presented at the Administrative Sciences Association of Canada Meeting at Dalhousie University, Halifax.

Kasl, S. 1974. "Work and Mental Health." In Work and Quality of Life: Resource Papers for Work in America, edited by James O'Toole, pp. 171-96. Cambridge, Mass.: MIT Press.

_____. 1973. "Mental Health and Work Environment: An Examination of the Evidence." Journal of Occupational Medicine 15: 509-18.

Kaufmann, W. 1970. "The Inevitability of Alienation." In Alienation, edited by Richard Schacht, pp. xiii-lvi. Garden City, N.Y.: Doubleday.

Kavanagh, M. J., A. C. Mackinney, and L. Wolins. 1971. "Issues in Managerial Performance: Multitrait-Multimethod Analysis of Ratings." Psychological Bulletin 75: 34-49.

Kimmons, S. G., and J. H. Greenhaus. 1976. "Relationship between Locus of Control and Reactions of Employees to Work Characteristics." Psychological Reports 39: 815-20.

Klein, E. 1966. A Comprehensive Etymological Dictionary of the English Language. New York: Elsevier.

Koch, J. L., and R. M. Steers. 1978. "Job Attachment, Satisfaction and Turnover among Public Sector Employees." Journal of Vocational Behavior 12: 119-28.

Kohn, M., and C. Schooler. 1969. "Class, Occupation, and Orientation." American Sociological Review 34: 659-78.

Korman, A. K., and R. W. Korman. 1980. Career Success/Personal Failure. Englewood Cliffs, N.J.: Prentice-Hall.

Kornhauser, A. 1965. Mental Health of the Industrial Worker: A Detroit Study. New York: Wiley.

Kurath, H., and S. M. Kuhn, eds. 1956. Middle English Dictionary. Ann Arbor: University of Michigan Press.

Lawler, E. E. 1973. Motivation in Work Organizations. Belmont, Calif.: Wadsworth.

_____. 1971. Pay and Organizational Effectiveness: A Psychological View. New York: McGraw-Hill.

_____. 1970. "Job Attitudes and Employee Motivation: Theory, Research, and Practice." Personnel Psychology 23: 223-37.

Lawler, E. E., and J. R. Hackman. 1971. "Corporate Profits and Employee Satisfaction: Must They Be in Conflict?" California Management Review 14: 46-55.

Lawler, E. E., and D. T. Hall. 1970. "Relationship of Job Characteristics to Job Involvement, Satisfaction, and Intrinsic Motivation." Journal of Applied Psychology 54: 305-12.

Lefkowitz, J. 1974. "Job Attitudes of Police: Overall Description and Demographic Correlates." Journal of Vocational Behavior 5: 221-30.

Levin, M. 1960. The Alienated Voter. New York: Holt, Rinehart and Winston.

Likert, R. 1961. New Patterns in Management. New York: McGraw-Hill.

Locke, J. 1947. "An Essay concerning the True Original, Extent and End of Civil Government." In Social Contract, edited by Ernest Barker, pp. 1-206. London: Oxford University Press.

Lodahl, T. M. 1964. "Patterns of Job Attitudes in Two Assembly Technologies." Administrative Science Quarterly 8: 482-515.

Lodahl, T. M., and M. Kejner. 1965. "The Definition and Measurement of Job Involvement." Journal of Applied Psychology 49: 24-33.

Lystad, M. H., ed. 1969. Social Aspects of Alienation: An Annotated Bibliography. Washington, D.C.: U.S. Government Printing Office.

McClelland, D. C. 1967. The Achieving Society. New York: Free Press.

McGregor, D. 1960. The Human Side of Enterprise. New York: McGraw-Hill.

McKelvey, B., and U. Sekaran. 1977. "Toward a Career-Based Theory of Job Involvement: A Study of Engineers and Scientists." Administrative Science Quarterly 22: 281-305.

McKinney, A. C., P. F. Wernimont, and W. O. Galitz. 1962. "Has Specialization Reduced Job Satisfaction?" Personnel 39: 8-17.

Macquarrie, J. 1973. "A Theology of Alienation." In Alienation: Concepts, Terms, and Meanings, edited by Frank Johnson, pp. 311-20. New York: Seminar Press.

Mannheim, B. 1975. "Comparative Study of Work Centrality, Job Rewards and Satisfaction: Occupational Groups in Israel." Sociology of Work and Occupations 5: 221-30.

Marx, K. 1963. Early Writings. Edited and translated by T. B. Bottomore. New York: McGraw-Hill.

_____. 1932. "Economic and Philosophical Manuscripts." In Marx-Engels Gesamtausgabe, vol. 3. Berlin: Marx-Engels Institute.

Maslow, A. H. 1954. Motivation and Personality. New York: Harper.

Maurer, J. 1969. Work Role Involvement of Industrial Supervisors. East Lansing: Michigan State University, Business Studies.

Mead, G. H. 1934. Mind, Self and Society. Chicago: University of Chicago Press.

Meissner, M. 1971. "The Long Arm of the Job: A Study of Work and Leisure." Industrial Relations 10: 239-60.

Merton, R. K. 1957. Social Theory and Social Structure. Glencoe, Ill.: Free Press.

Middleton, R. 1963. "Alienation, Race, and Education." American Sociological Review 28: 973-77.

Miller, G. A. 1967. "Professionals in Bureaucracy: Alienation among Industrial Scientists and Engineers." American Sociological Review 32: 755-68.

Mills, C. W. 1951. White Collar. New York: Oxford University Press.

Misra, S., and A. Kalro. 1981. "Job Involvement of Intrinsically and Extrinsically Motivated Indian Managers: To Each According to His Need." Human Relations 34: 419-26.

Mitchell, V. F., V. V. Baba, and T. Epps. 1975. "On the Relationship between Job Involvement and Central Life Interest." Relations industrielles 30: 166-80.

Moch, M. K. 1980. "Job Involvement, Internal Motivation, and Employees' Integration into Networks of Work Relationships." Organizational Behavior and Human Performance 25: 15-31.

Morse, N. C., and R. S. Weiss. 1955. "The Function and Meaning of Work and the Job." American Sociological Review 20: 191-98.

Mukherjee, B. N. 1969. "Interrelationships among Measures of Job Satisfaction and Job Involvement." Indian Journal of Psychology 44: 21-32.

Murray, J. A., ed. 1888. New English Dictionary on Historical Principles. Oxford: Clarendon Press.

Nakane, C. 1970. Japanese Society. Berkeley and Los Angeles: University of California Press.

Neal, A., and S. Rettig. 1963. "Dimensions of Alienation among Manual Workers and Non-Manual Workers." American Sociological Review 28: 599-608.

Newman, J. E. 1975. "Understanding Organizational Structure—Job Attitude Relationship through Perceptions of the Work Environment." Organizational Behavior and Human Performance 13: 371-79.

Nisbet, R. 1953. The Quest for Community. New York: Oxford University Press.

Oates, W. E. 1971. Confessions of a Workaholic. Cleveland: World.

Osgood, C. E., G. J. Suci, and P. H. Tannenbaum. 1957. The Measurement of Meaning. Urbana: University of Illinois Press.

Parker, S. 1971. The Future of Work and Leisure. New York: Praeger.

Patchen, M. 1970. Participation, Achievement and Involvement on the Job. Englewood Cliffs, N.J.: Prentice-Hall.

Quinn, R. P., S. E. Seashore, R. L. Kahn, T. Mangione, D. Campbell, G. Staines, and M. McCullough. 1971. Survey of Working Conditions. Washington, D.C.: U.S. Government Printing Office.

Rabinowitz, S. 1975. "An Examination of the Influence of Individual Difference Variables and Perceived Job Stimulation on Job Involvement." Unpublished master's thesis, Michigan State University.

Rabinowitz, S., and D. T. Hall. 1977. "Organizational Research on Job Involvement." Psychological Bulletin 84: 265-88.

Rabinowitz, S., D. T. Hall, and J. G. Goodale. 1977. "Job Scope and Individual Differences as Predictors of Job Involvement: Independent or Interactive?" Academy of Management Journal 20: 273-81.

Rousseau, D. M. 1978. "Measures of Technology as Predictors of Employee Attitude." Journal of Applied Psychology 63: 213-18.

Rousseau, J. 1947. "The Social Contract." In Social Contract, edited by Ernest Barker, pp. 237–440. London: Oxford University Press.

Rotter, J. B. 1966. "Generalized Expectancies for Internal versus External Control of Reinforcement." Psychological Monographs, vol. 80, no. 1 (whole no. 609).

Ruh, R. A., R. G. Johnson, and P. M. Scontrino. 1973. "The Scanlon Plan: Participation in Decision Making and Job Attitudes." Journal of Industrial and Organizational Psychology 1: 36–45.

Ruh, R. A., J. K. White, and R. R. Wood. 1975. "Job Involvement, Values, Personal Background, Participation in Decision Making and Job Attitudes." Academy of Management Journal 18: 300–12.

Runyon, K. 1973. "Some Interactions between Personality Variables and Management Styles." Journal of Applied Psychology 57: 288–94.

Saal, F. E. 1981. "Empirical and Theoretical Implications of a Purely Cognitive Definition of Job Involvement." International Review of Applied Psychology 30: 103–20.

_____. 1978. "Job Involvement: A Multivariate Approach." Journal of Applied Psychology 63: 53–61.

Saleh, S. D. 1981. "A Structural View of Job Involvement and Its Differentiation from Satisfaction and Motivation." International Review of Applied Psychology 30: 17–29.

_____. 1971. "Development of Job Attitude Scale." Department of Management Science, University of Waterloo. Mimeographed.

_____. 1964. "A Study of Attitude Change in the Pre-Retirement Period." Journal of Applied Psychology 48: 310–12.

Saleh, S. D., and J. Hosek. 1976. "Job Involvement: Concepts and Measurements." Academy of Management Journal 19: 213–24.

Schacht, R. 1970. Alienation. Garden City, N.J.: Doubleday.

Schiller, F. 1954. On the Aesthetic Education of Man, in a Series of Letters. Translated by Reginald Snell. New Haven, Conn.: Yale University Press.

Schneider, B. , D. T. Hall, and H. T. Nygren. 1971. "Self Image and Job Characteristics as Correlates of Changing Organizational Identification." Human Relations 24: 397-416.

Schuler, R. S. 1975. "Determinants of Job Involvement: Individual versus Organizational: An Extension of the Literature." Paper presented at the Academy of Management Meeting in New Orleans.

Schwyhart, N. R. , and P. C. Smith. 1972. "Factors in the Job Involvement of Middle Managers." Journal of Applied Psychology 56: 227-33.

Seeman, M. 1975. "Alienation Studies." Annual Review of Sociology 1: 91-123.

_____. 1971. "The Urban Alienation: Some Dubious Theses from Marx to Marcuse." Journal of Personality and Social Psychology 19: 135-43.

_____. 1967. "On the Personal Consequences of Alienation in Work." American Sociological Review 32: 273-85.

_____. 1959. "On the Meaning of Alienation." American Sociological Review 24: 783-91.

Shepard, J. M. 1971. Automation and Alienation: A Study of Office and Factory Workers. Cambridge, Mass.: MIT Press.

Siegel, A. L. 1971. "Antecedents and Consequences of Job Involvement." Unpublished master's thesis, Michigan State University.

_____. 1969. Industrial Psychology. Homewood, Ill.: Irvine.

Siegel, A. L. , and R. A. Ruh. 1973. "Job Involvement, Participation in Decision Making, Personal Background and Job Behavior." Organizational Behavior and Human Performance 9: 318-29.

SleeSmith, P. I. 1973. Job Involvement and Communications. London: Business Books.

Smith, A. 1937. An Inquiry into the Nature and Causes of the Wealth of Nations. New York: Modern Library.

Steers, R. M. 1981. Introduction to Organizational Behavior. Santa Monica, Calif.: Goodyear.

_____. 1976. "Factors Affecting Job Attitudes in a Goal Setting Environment." Academy of Management Journal 19: 6-16.

_____. 1975. "Effects of Need for Achievement on the Job Performance—Job Attitude Relationship." Journal of Applied Psychology 60: 678-82.

Steers, R. M., and D. W. Braunstein. 1976. "Behaviorally Based Measure of Manifest Needs in Work Settings." Journal of Vocational Behavior 9: 251-66.

Susman, G. I. 1973. "Job Enlargement: Effects of Culture on Worker Responses." Industrial Relations 12: 1-15.

Sykes, A. J. M. 1965. "Some Differences in the Attitudes of Clerical and Manual Workers." Sociological Review 13: 297-310.

Tannenbaum, A. 1966. Social Psychology of the Work Organization. Belmont, Calif.: Brooks/Cole.

Taylor, F. W. 1911. Principles of Scientific Management. New York: Harper & Bros.

Taylor, R. N., and M. Thompson. 1976. "Work Value Systems of Young Workers." Academy of Management Journal 19: 522-36.

Torbert, W. R., and M. P. Rogers. 1973. Being for the Most Part Puppets. Cambridge, Mass.: Schenkman.

Tocqueville, Alexis de. 1961. Democracy in America, vol. 2. New York: Shocken Books.

Trist, E. L., and K. W. Bamforth. 1951. "Some Social and Psychological Consequences of the Longwall Method of Goal-Getting." Human Relations 4: 3-38.

Vroom, V. H. 1969. "Industrial Social Psychology." In The Handbook of Social Psychology, edited by G. Lindzey and E. Aronson, vol. 5, 2d ed., pp. 196-268. Reading, Mass.: Addison-Wesley.

_____. 1964. Work and Motivation. New York: Wiley.

_____. 1962. "Ego Involvement, Job Satisfaction, and Job Performance." Personnel Psychology 15: 159-77.

Walker, C. R., and R. H. Guest. 1952. The Man on the Assembly Line. Cambridge, Mass.: Harvard University Press.

Walton, R. E. 1972. "How to Counter Alienation in the Plant." Harvard Business Review 50 (November-December): 70-81.

Wanous, J. P. 1974. "Individual Differences and Reactions to Job Characteristics." Journal of Applied Psychology 59: 616-22.

Warr, P., J. Cook, and T. Wall. 1979. "Scales for the Measurement of Some Work Attitudes and Aspects of Psychological Well-being." Journal of Occupational Psychology 52: 129-48.

Waters, L. K., D. Roach, and N. Batlis. 1974. "Organizational Climate Dimensions and Job-Related Attitudes." Personnel Psychology 27: 465-76.

Weber, M. 1930. The Protestant Ethic and the Spirit of Capitalism. London: George Allen and Unwin.

Weiss, D. J. 1976. "Multivariate Procedures." In Handbook of Industrial and Organizational Psychology, edited by Marvin D. Dunnette, pp. 327-62. Chicago: Rand McNally.

Weissenberg, P., and L. Gruenfeld. 1968. "Relationship between Job Satisfaction and Job Involvement." Journal of Applied Psychology 52: 469-73.

White, J. K. 1978. "Generalizability of Individual Difference Moderators of the Participation in Decision Making—Employee Response Relationship." Academy of Management Journal 21: 36-43.

White, J. K., and R. A. Ruh. 1973. "Effects of Personal Values on the Relationship between Participation and Job Attitudes." Administrative Science Quarterly 18: 506-14.

Wickert, F. R. 1951. "Turnover and Employee Feeling of Ego Involvement in the Day-to-Day Operations of a Company." Personnel Psychology 4: 185-97.

Wiener, Y., and A. S. Gechman. 1977. "Commitment: A Behavioral Approach to Job Involvement." Journal of Vocational Behavior 10: 47-62.

Wilensky, H. L. 1961. "Life Cycle, Work Situation, and Participation in Formal Associations." In Aging and Leisure: A Research Perspective into the Meaningful Use of Time, edited by R. W. Kleemeier, pp. 213-42. New York: Oxford University Press.

Wollack, S., J. G. Goodale, J. P. Wijting, and P. C. Smith. 1971. "Development of the Survey of Work Values." Journal of Applied Psychology 55: 331-38.

Wood, D. A. 1971. "Enhancing Attitude-Performance Relationships by Degree of Job Involvement." Proceedings of the American Psychological Association, annual meeting, pp. 495-96.

INDEX

ABOUT THE AUTHOR

RABINDRA N. KANUNGO is a professor of psychology and management at McGill University, Montreal, Canada. Before coming to McGill in 1969, he was an associate professor of psychology at Dalhousie University, Halifax, Canada.

Dr. Kanungo has published widely in both the basic and applied areas of psychology and management. His publications include more than 50 professional articles in such journals as the Journal of Experimental Psychology, the Journal of Applied Psychology, the Journal of Personality and Social Psychology, Organizational Behavior and Human Performance, Psychological Bulletin, and so on. He is the coauthor of Memory and Affect: A Reformulation (Pergamon 1975) and a coeditor of Behavioral Issues in Management: The Canadian Context (McGraw-Hill Ryerson 1977). His most recent book is Biculturalism and Management (Butterworths 1980).

Dr. Kanungo received his B.A. (Honours in Philosophy) and M.A. degrees in India and his Ph.D. from McGill University, Canada. His work experience as a university professor, researcher, and consultant spans both East (India) and West (Canada and the United States). His academic and professional honors include a Commonwealth Fellowship, a Seagram Fellowship, and a Fellowship of the Canadian Psychological Association.